St. Willibrord Studies
in Philosophy and Religion
ISSN 1059-8375
Number Five

I0151869

THE MYSTIC PATH

by
Bishop Karl Prüter

BORGO PRESS / WILDSIDE PRESS

www.wildsidepress.com

* * * * * * * *

Copyright © 1997 by Bishop Karl Pruter

Library of Congress Cataloging-in-Publication Data

Pruter, Karl, 1920-
  The mystic path / by Karl Pruter.
    p. cm. — (St. Willibrord studies in philosophy and religion, ISSN 1059-
8375 ; no. 5)
  Includes bibliographical references and index.
  ISBN 0-912134-32-1 (cloth). — ISBN 0-912134-33-X (pbk.)
  1. Mysticism. 2. Spiritual life—Old Catholic Church. I. Title. II. Series.
BV5082.2.P78 1997   96-48219
248.2'2—dc21   CIP

FIRST EDITION

CONTENTS

INTRODUCTION

Many theologians believe that mysticism cannot be set down in a systematic theological form. The faith of the mystics is thought to be such a fragile thing that it disintegrates if one attempts to explain it in theological terms. This is not so. Mysticism is far from a fragile belief, but what happens is that it ceases to be alive and vital when it is set forth simply as belief. For mysticism is essentially an experiential faith. It is not what one believes about God, but rather what one does with Him that really matters. The value of theology to Christianity is overrated. Theologians contribute little to spiritual growth and progress. At best, they record the footprints of those who have pioneered in traveling new paths.

Further, one cannot understand Christianity until one meets Christ, Who is the best known of the mystics. If one wants to understand mystical Christianity, it is better to seek out a saint than to seek out a theologian. In the chapters that follow, I present to you not theology, but an essential experiential mysticism through a guide to prayer in the first half of the book, and a number of devotional prayers in the second half, "Prayers of the Mystical Way." The first five chapters are written to help you understand what you are asking when you come to the King of the Universe and ask for "An Awakening, Purgation, Illumination, and Union with Him." The prayers presented can be your mystical path to God.

I do not offer rote prayers that by some magical process will obtain for those who recite them the Kingdom of Heaven. Jesus cautioned us against such rote repetition of prayers, but the same Jesus promised that when a man came before God and seriously besought Him, God would answer his petitions. Therefore, it behooves us to ask wisely, and to understand what it is we wish to receive. One can hardly pray for a resolve to serve God, that is, for an "awakening," without knowing what is involved. This is especially so once we learn that those who have experienced such an awakening underwent a change in lifestyle, and thought that there was no possibility of turning back.

Their lives were marked by a new goal and a new passion, that of uniting themselves with God. This Union with God was the reward for their total commitment to Him, what Jesus referred to as "A pearl of great price." You are invited to read what I have written, and as you come to understand each step in the mystical path, I ask that you offer the prayers for each step, for by so doing, you become not just a reader of the Word, but also a doer. The mystics say that God created you in order that you might come into Union with Him. I hope to explain why you must seek Union with God, and to help you along the mystical path so that you might achieve that Blessed Union.

—Bishop Karl Pruter
Highlandville, Missouri
Transfiguration Day, 1995

I.

MYSTICISM

War...crime...poverty...disease, and death! These are the principal problems for which mankind seeks a solution. The search is unrelenting, and we seem to get no nearer to any solution as the centuries roll by. Yet, two thousand years ago Jesus of Nazareth offered his hearers a new Kingdom, which he promised his hearers would bring life abundant and life eternal. That He offered it would not matter, except for the following facts.

First, He Himself conquered death. He lives and He daily communicates with thousands upon thousands of his followers.

Second, those of his followers who have taken his words literally have also gained victory over death. They have found the Kingdom where war, poverty, crime, disease, and death have been banished. These people are the mystics, and the theology which they espouse goes under various names: most commonly, contemplative theology or mystical theology. They have offered it as a solution to the problems of the world, and because the world continues to reject their solution, they divorce themselves from the world and its governments.

They give their allegiance to one kingdom, the Kingdom of God. They do not seek to impose this kingdom upon the rest of the world or upon other people. But they do claim that it is part of God's plan for man, which He intended at our creation. They also say it is the only way that makes sense, and it is the only way that conforms to reality. When you ask them to prove it, or even to prove the God upon which their ideas are based, they decline.

"God," they say, "Is indefinable and unprovable." Instead, they do, as Jesus did, invite men to come and taste.

Mysticism is an experimental science which seeks to help men remove the mountain of self that stands between God and men. Or more simply put: a mystic is one who seeks to unite with God. This definition is at once both exciting and audacious. But Meister Eckhart, a fourteenth-century mystic, phrased it most reasonably when he said, "God became man in order that man might become God." I say reasonably, yet down through the ages those who have represented the religious Establishment have deemed such talk as madness. But unless man can become like God, what hope is there for man? Who can look at the world about him and have any hope that man can resolve the age-old problems of war, poverty, and oppression? Since the turn of the century we have actually lost some of the ground we had gained in the previous centuries.

Rather than cope with the problems confronting us, we have copped out. Led by the existentialist philosophers, the world has chosen not to apply reason and science to spiritual matters, but has opted to set them aside in religion, in art, music, and philosophy. By the middle of the century, many people were beginning to sense that something was wrong. It was the countercultural generation of the 1960s that seemed to sense it first, and it was these individuals who were willing to face up to the fact that twentieth-century man was headed in the wrong direction, and ultimately to his own destruction. The explosive '60s were to a large extent a blind response by young people striking out at a sick society. Thousands turned their backs on the establishment and sought answers in exotic cults, astrology, ancient religions, and even witchcraft. In rejecting contemporary society, this generation made sweeping denunciations. They found fault with the political and economic structure. They saw organized religion as repressive. Religion was denounced by some because they felt it supported the establishment, and by others because their parents professed values which they did not live. Typical of those who rejected the faith of their parents were many young Jewish people who sought out Jews for Jesus, the Hare Krishnas, and the Mooneys.

Oddly enough, the young people of this era experienced great material progress, which they realized had been achieved over centuries in a slow, uphill, and cumulative progression. They rejected what they called "materialism," although many of their numbers continued to accept the support of their parents as they pursued their anti-establishment lifestyle. They failed to see that society had not only produced great material advancements in the form of an increased food supply and the ability of people, at least in the first world, to provide man's basic needs without working from sunrise to sunset, but that there had also been much moral and spiritual growth. Not only did they fail to see this growth, but they often falsely concluded that we had declined almost from the day man had left the caves.

To the sixties generation, no credit was given to religion, particularly Christianity, for having ended such ancient practices as those which permitted a Roman father to kill his children, or the institution of slavery, or abortion. Actually, it was the call for freedom during the sixties that brought back the widespread use of abortion as a form of birth control.

But mankind had indeed made progress in the spiritual realm. If we study history carefully, we will see that each great period of artistic, material, and intellectual activity brought with it a new wave of men and women who explored the spiritual universe, and who reported new findings, or new confirmations of old truths.

During the great Classical Period of mysticism, the fourteenth century, mystics appeared and charted the spiritual world even as cartographers charted the physical world. The same dual activity marked the Medieval and Renaissance periods of history. Most significantly during the fourteenth century, man experienced a spiritual breakthrough, but he did not pursue this assiduously. Had he done so, the world would have taken a different course. Unfortunately, the Renaissance brought discoveries in the physical world which diverted man's attention from spiritual things.

The most towering figure of the early fourteenth century was a Dominican priest known as Meister Eckhart. He was born Johannes Eckhart in a small village in Germany, Hochheim, about 1260. He was followed by two other mystics, Johannes Tauler and Heinrich Süse. These three individuals taught men to explore new spiritual frontiers, and it seemed as if a new age of discovery was about to be ushered in. At the same time, other men were exploring the outer limits of the physical world, both in science and geography. Since the exploration of the physical world appears less demanding, it became more popular, and with the coming of the Renaissance, man devoted the overwhelming bulk of his energies and resources to the exploration of the material world about him.

The twentieth century comes across as the century of materialism, when actually it has been a century of considerable spiritual progress. It is an age that has given us Kahlil Gibran, Mahatma Gandhi, Charles Foucauld, Mother Teresa of Calcutta, and Thomas Merton. The Roman Catholic monk, Thomas Merton, in time will be the most studied, the best known, and the most imitated mystic of all time. I say this only because he lived in an age where every movement and every word of this living saint in our midst could be recorded and was recorded. His superiors, in fact, were fearful that this over exposure of Merton would prevent him from ever being acknowledged as a saint. After all, what do we know about the clay feet of any of the great mystics, such as Augustine, John of the Cross, or Jacob Boehme, except what they chose to confess?

We have to keep in mind that their sins, which they confessed, come to us complete with their interpretations and explanations for them. Thomas Merton's sins, on the other hand, are written about by his friends and contemporaries. Although he spent years in a Trappist monastery, where normally things are kept hidden, his life was an open book. First, he became a celebrity through his life and writing, and secondly, this was an age of unusual openness. As we read about Merton, we are tempted to let our imagination soar and visualize a monk peering over his prayer bench and reading, "Smile, you're on *Candid Camera.*" But Merton survived this exposure, which should be quite heartening, since, it shows that a mystic is not just a creation of the Church's public relations department, but that he does exist. Not only do mystics exist, but they are honest, sincere, and truly holy men of God.

The present spiritual explosion did not come about because the mystics were persuasive, but for totally negative reasons. The Vietnam War, and the failure of modern society to solve its social, economic, and political problems, convinced a generation that the answer must lie outside the material world of the senses. The modern church was so identified with the established society, that it failed to offer an option for those seeking an alternative culture. The Church, accustomed to being rejected as otherworldly, was finally rejected because she *was* worldly. Suburban religion in particular seemed dedicated to creating and preserving a material way of life that offered all the social and economic amenities, but little place for piety, devotional life, meditation, and the simple ascetic life.

To the suburbanite, "the ascetic life" had no appeal, and was seen as some kind of perverse abnormality. Hence, when the "hip" generation sought spiritual solace, it deliberately chose those forms that least resembled twentieth-century western capitalist society. It was not just a protest. It was simply that, if an alternative lifestyle was to be found, it did not seem likely that it would be found in the established religious institutions. In the rush to find spiritual alternatives, the public turned to the East, and many fruitful contacts were made between Eastern and Western teachers.

Notable was Thomas Merton's voyage to the Orient and his meetings with the Dalai Lama. But it also opened the door for charlatans and peculiar cults. A guru who could not attract a following in India could often come to America and pick up a sizable following of lost souls. Astrologers, psychics, and even witches gained an audience and found adherents. The holocaust at People's Temple in Jonestown was the result of an uncritical search of a frustrated generation. Shortly thereafter, the new cults from the East and their home-grown varieties seemed to cease their growth and many of them went into decline.

Now, thirty years later, the New Age Movement seems to have gained a new lease on life and is again attracting new followers. In addition, a few solid, mostly older historic Eastern religions have found a home in the West, and the traditional spirituality of the Western Church is continuing its twentieth-century re-emergence. In part this is due to the work of Thomas Merton, which in turn was stimulated by the sixties revolution and the New Age challenge. I suspect that Thomas Merton will probably be recognized as the most important figure of the first half of the twentieth century.

One of the paradoxes of our time is that much of the interest in Merton, at least in the beginning, took place outside of the Catholic Church. The Roman Church at Vatican II placed its bets in the wrong corner. It did everything possible to shed its otherworldly image, and shifted from encouraging the contemplative life to encouraging the activist life. The nuns shed their habits and got into miniskirts, and the guitar became the church instrument of preference. Mind you, this was taking place while thousands of young people were turning to communes and to Eastern cults that used colorful, very otherworldly, and very nonwestern habits. Guitars were exchanged for sitars and oriental gongs. The Church, which for nearly two thousand years has been trying to bring men and women to participate in various forms of meditation, ceased to place much importance on the contemplative life. Priests are no longer required to read the breviary daily, and cloisters and monasteries of various contemplative orders have been closed.

One of the strangest paradoxes was the inability of the Church to recruit new people to the contemplative monasteries and cloisters. They offered meditation freely and without price and found no takers in the modern world, and the assumption was that the Church had to have a new focus. But what the Church couldn't give away, Maharishi Mahesh Yogi was able to sell to a generation that was hungry for a meditative life. Transcendental Meditation (TM)

12

was quickly accepted, not only in the "hippie" communes, but by corporations willing to pay good money to have it taught to their executives. The Church has always been accused of being financially astute, and at times of selling salvation. Even in the heyday of peddling indulgences, the Church never prospered like Scientology, Transcendental Meditation, and even the Divine Light Mission. I am not concerned about the prosperity of the cults, but I want to call attention to the evident demand for that which the Church cannot give away.

But the Church should have known better. It should have asked itself, "Why did Thomas Merton's books sell so well?" Eventually, of course, the Church will awaken to what it has in Merton, and, fortunately, by that time he will have become public property. I believe we are at the threshold of a new age of mysticism, fully as vital and influential as that of the fourteenth century. Modern man has explored the universe and has found it wanting. He has explored his own mind, and has not liked what he has discovered about himself. He is now beginning the search for ultimate reality. In a sense, he is returning to the source, the Creator of the universe. The paths are many, and there is a confusing cacophony of sound and voices clamoring for our attention. This may be an important reason for considering the teachings of the Western Mystics. They have been around for a long time, they have been well studied, and the way they have taught has been tried and tested by literally thousands. More importantly, their claims have been studied, tried, and tested, and not found wanting. For this reason, in the competition with the New Age religions, I believe, the teachings of the classical mystics will become the household faith and beliefs of twenty-first-century man. One reason for believing that mysticism will become the faith of the next century is based on the simplicity of their method.

The classical mystics did not believe that union with God was reserved for the intelligent, for people with secret knowledge, or for any other elitist group. They taught that God was most apt to seek out simple men and women.

They taught that God looked into the hearts of men and would return tenfold any love that He found there.

This is not to say that He avoids intellectuals, for many mystics could be labeled as such; but rather that there was no particular man or woman that was more capable of finding God than any other. Before God all men are equal. Unfortunately, if He gives more talent to some men and women, they are apt to let pride in their abilities hinder their approach to God. Hence, we are admonished to humble ourselves, and to allow God in his own way to find us. Many people who complain that God is elusive are in reality fleeing from Him.

But to all who seek Him and are willing to prepare a place for Him, God promises to enter into their hearts. It is a fourfold process: first of all, it is an awakening or conviction. Second comes purification. Third is enlightenment or illumination. Finally, there is union with God.

Awakening resembles what the Evangelicals call "conversion." However, it is not the acceptance of beliefs or the exchange of one set of ideas for another. Rather, it is a move from self-centeredness to God-centeredness. Hence, an individual who once was satisfied to relate every experience and every phenomenon to himself, now seeks to relate himself to the One Great Absolute, God! Before this revelation, the self and self-survival were the center of the soul's existence, and its one great driving force: suddenly, these cease to matter and are of no concern to the awakened individual.

From this point on, the formerly self-centered individual becomes obsessed in his desire to find God and to achieve oneness with Him. He seeks neither to save himself, nor merely to find himself, but literally to lose himself in God.

Mystical literature is filled with stories, many of them spectacular, of how individuals have experienced this awakening. However, not all mystics have had a sudden or a traumatic awakening. In many instances this experience came about almost imperceptibly over the years. But let me stress—it did come about, and there was a watershed experience. There was a time, dramatic or undramatic, when the person made a one-hundred-and-eighty-degree turn, and it marked the beginning of his march to take the Kingdom of God by storm. Yet, no matter how simply the awakening comes, it is almost invariably followed by a period of great stress. Jesus Christ, Saint Paul, and others fled into the desert to think and meditate concerning the meaning of their awakening experience. It is a period of temptation and sometimes of confusion. The temptation to use one's new insight for selfish ends is most noticeable at the time of awakening. The confusion is easy to imagine. For some, the values and habits of an entire lifetime have to be left behind, and a new lifestyle has to be learned to take the place of the old and familiar.

The awakening of Ignatius Loyola, a young Italian soldier in the sixteenth century, was simple and clear, yet left the convert very confused. He had suffered an injury and during his long recovery period he had read much about Christ and the early saints. Shortly after he was out riding one day and saw the trees budding, a phenomenon that he had witnessed many times before. This time, however, he saw not budding trees, but the hand of God the Creator at work. His experience convinced him that soldiering was not a suitable occupation for one who is aware of the Living God. He asked himself, "How can I serve Him?" All he knew was the military life, and it was what he was trained to do. He needed to pray and meditate for many months before he understood that God could use his soldierly talents and skills in a new and different kind of warfare. He would serve the Church in winning back many of the souls that had been lost to Her as a result of the turmoil of the Protestant Reformation which was then sweeping Europe.

For another, like Jacob Boehme, there was the necessity of learning a new skill. He was a cobbler who mended the soles of shoes, and now he would mend the souls of men. First he needed to learn to write. And write he did, and learned men from all over Europe flocked to his cobbler's shop to talk with him and to pour over his manuscripts. The awakening is in itself a learning experience, but learning for the mystic comes mainly in the third step of the mystical experience, namely the illumination. But between the awakening and the illumination is the step called purgation, which St. John of the Cross so aptly called, "The Dark Night of the Soul."

Purgation follows naturally from the awakening, for it no sooner seizes a man and turns him to God than his thoughts cause him to reconsider his condition. It is as if a man were told of a great treasure that awaited him, if only he would pursue it with all his strength, with all his mind and will. No thought of danger, hardship, or any other consideration can deter him from seeking his goal. He must pursue it, even though he knows that once he had not been disturbed by the thought, for its existence to him was then unknown; but now that he knows of it, he cannot enjoy his former peace, but must risk all because of what he has learned. What he has learned is that God is a reality that he can know. Further, God claims us as his sons and daughters, and asks us to seek Union with Him.

It is at this point that the awakened one is excited and challenged by the glimpse of what awaits him, and so he is sickened by the awareness of his own shortcomings. He does not and cannot feel worthy enough to stand in the presence of God; and yet, he now knows that he is being invited to seek union with his Creator.

He also must be conscious of the fact that for every mystic called by God, there have been a hundred "loonies" with illusions of grandeur and with psychotic pretensions. Then, of course, doubt rears its ugly head, and he wonders if the experience of awakening is for real. Perhaps it is these doubts that bring the aspirant to the next step of purification. For an awakened individual has to be aware that God does not unite with dross, but with other gold, equally refined and free of dross. Before he can become a fit habitation for God, he must prepare himself by purging his soul of all that hinders or prevents his union with God.

Purgation is the longest and most difficult step in the mystical path. It may take years, and end in discouragement and failure. It brings with it a flood of doubts, temptations, and frustrations. As we read the *Confessions of Jacob Boehme* and the *Confessions of Saint Augustine*, we are struck by how their failures, even those we might regard as trifling, bring them acute pain and suffering. The whole process of purgation is truly the "dark night of the soul." It involves not merely living some ethical code or standard, but complete and total purity of heart and mind. It means not just doing good, but more importantly, being good. The designation "holy man" or "holy woman" is accurate. In a sense, it means a person who has become incapable of doing or thinking evil. It means never having feelings that are not in harmony with the spirit of God. Purgation involves several clearly defined steps. First, there must be detachment from the sensual things that bind the soul to earth. Second, there must be mortification, or the process of finding a positive, newfound energy. A life of Christian action necessarily follows. The soul, having forsaken earthly things, must now become all absorbed in spiritual things. This may consist of constant prayer, or it may include suffering and self-inflicted asceticism, which some have carried to extremes.

Purgation may end in Illumination, in which the mystic is given new direction and new tasks. There is a tendency for purgation and illumination to overlap. Indeed, it seems difficult for anyone to come through the purgation stage without the help of illumination. Orthodox Catholicism insists that a man is saved by grace or illumination, which is a gift of God. The emphasis is not on man's reaching upward to God, but upon God reaching down to man. Whatever the interpretation, illumination seems to spur the mystic by giving him a glimpse into the future—an awareness of what awaits him at the end of the road of purgation.

Illumination, sometimes called cosmic consciousness, is simply the sense of the presence of God in an ecstatic, almost hallucinatory state. These illuminations are often accompanied by flashes of insight, and are extremely productive periods for those who receive them. A simple, poorly-educated man like William Blake, an eighteenth-century English mystic, amazed the world with his production of both great literature and great art.

All the mystics, without exception, have been highly productive people. All have been men and women of tremendous insight—insight which in many cases seemed to exceed the ability of mortal men and women. St. Teresa of Avila fought kings and bishops, and established monasteries throughout Spain at a time when women were supposed to listen and follow the lead of their superiors, who were most often men. The illumination of the mystics has been examined and explained away by their critics in terms of their vitality, or even their self-deception; but their amazing accomplishments are there and cannot be explained away. Jacob Boehme, the simple shoemaker with almost no education, wrote volumes that brought educated men from all over Europe to read his manuscripts and to question him in order that they might learn. There were too many mystics, like Boehme and Blake, and they accomplished too much for everything to be brought to naught by the glib phrase, the pat explanation, or the Freudian rationalizing of the obvious.

Let us examine together the mystical four-fold path, and discover for ourselves the world of the spirit which they discovered, and in which the great mystics dwelt for the greater part of their lives. Let us also, as we read the chapters on the awakening, purgation, illumination, and union with God, pray the prayers intended to take us through the same steps which produced God's mystics. Only in this way can we understand and evaluate the lives and the accomplishments of the mystics. Although men do not agree that all of their accomplishments were divinely inspired, all are agreed that there has to be some explanation for the tremendous outpouring of literary and artistic work which mysticism inspired. There is something unique in the life of the mystic that makes him unusually creative.

To follow in this path will take some courage and resolve on your part. First, because the mystics say you must let go of the life you have known and in which you have felt secure for all of your past years. Second, it must be admitted that the mystics have always skated close to that line which separates orthodoxy from heterodoxy, and in the final step, "union with God" they frequently came close to the edge. Yet, Jesus Christ promised that He would make all his followers joint heirs with him in the Kingdom of God, since, he claimed with God, if we are to be joint heirs, we cannot become less than the Sons of God. St. Athanasius said of Jesus, "He became man that we might be made God." That a Church Father said this was fortunate, for many of the mystics have often cited him as an authority when they repeated it. Eckhart claimed to be following the Church Fathers when he wrote, "Our Lord says to every living soul, 'I became man for you. If you do not become God for me, you do me wrong.'" The claim, however, did not go unchallenged. Eckhart was declared a heretic posthumously and many of the mystics were constantly suspected of heresy, and their works were often banned and subsequently burned.

The idea that man can have Union with God is daring. Yet, it is rational, and therefore intelligent people cannot reject an idea simply because it is daring. Nor can it be rejected because it is stated with the passion of one who has just emerged from an ecstatic experience. We have to examine carefully the evidence of the mystical experiences and of the mystics, and then draw our conclusions. If we examine fairly the writings of the mystics and the critical comments of their contemporaries, we shall probably have to conclude that their claims are justified, or at the very least, conclude that we are incapable of passing judgment. Often we find ourselves in the position of those who listened to the seemingly wild tales of travelers to Cathay or to the New World. We are skeptical, but until we ourselves have traveled where they have gone, we cannot say with certainty that what they claimed to have seen and experienced is or is not true!

To sum up this introduction, let me say that I am aware of one basic weakness in the mystical answer to the world's problems. It is too simple! People in Jesus's day were angered and crucified Him, not because He did not have the answer, but because He did. The answer He offers throws the responsibility right back on us. What Jesus and the mystics are saying is offensive to a lot of people.

They say, "If you don't like the world, shape up and get in harmony with God's plan. Become a part of the Kingdom of God and you shall know life abundant and life eternal. Reject it and continue to wallow in the hell you yourself have helped create." Before you reject their uncompromising and absolutist position, I would like to suggest that you do some experimental work and actually try their methods of meditation and the four-fold path of classical mysticism.

Beginning with the next chapter, "The Awakening," read thoughtfully and prayerfully. As you read, turn to Chapter VI and pray the prayers of Awakening. Do the same for the chapters on "Purgation," "Illumination," and "Union with God." For each step use the appropriate prayers, keeping in mind the axiom that, "A perfect prayer bringeth forth a perfect answer, and an imperfect prayer bringeth forth an imperfect answer." Remember, God wants to answer these prayers as much, nay more, than you desire that they be answered. "For God," say Christ and the mystics, "is seeking men and women who desire Him." You have been offered the Pearl of Great Price. If you try and fail, at least you will better understand the mystics and the world in which they had their life and being. But, if you sincerely seek Union with God, you cannot fail, for God has offered to receive unto Himself all those who seek him in spirit and in truth.

Read on, my friend, and become one of the mystics!

II.

THE AWAKENING

Perhaps it is far easier to understand how the Atheist allowed self to blot out a vision of God, than what moved him to undertake a search for God in the first place. How and when are we awakened to the realization that He is, or even that He might be?

At the beginning of this book, I defined mysticism and then I defined a mystic. A mystic is someone who seeks union with the cosmos (*i.e.*, God). In every age mystics abound, and in ever-increasing numbers. However, even today they constitute such a small minority of people, that one must ask the question, why? If this way is, as the mystics claim, the only route by which man can comprehend the universe and serve the purpose for which he was created, why does it seem to be reserved for so few?

One answer of the mystics is: there is no good reason to ask why. Rather, we should accept the fact that this is a rare pearl of great value, and reach out and take it. Another response is that this is the end product of man's evolutionary development! In ancient times few men achieved this union with the cosmos, but as man has evolved, his spiritual senses have developed, and more men have undertaken the search for the Ultimate. In time, we are told, everyone will attempt to reach out and seek union with God. But whatever the reason, we have to deal with the fact that the search for God is the pre-occupation of a very few gifted and talented men and women. Let us remember that the world's best-known mystic, Jesus Christ, chose only twelve intimate disciples. This is hardly a number one would seek out to begin a world revolutionary

21

movement. Yet, even Jesus thought that what he had to impart was best given to a chosen few.

If you read the *New Testament* carefully, you will find that Jesus often refers to the blind. Now it is true that the Middle East in his day and even in ours abounds with blind people, but Jesus often refers to sighted people as being "blind." He talks of people, "Who have eyes, but who do not see." If you want to learn what he felt caused this spiritual blindness, you have only to note the people who wanted to join his movement whom he turned away. Some who came had many possessions which blinded them to spiritual truth and he sent them away. One young man was too pre-occupied with the care of his father, and Jesus simply told him, "Let the dead bury the dead." Jesus apparently regarded the young man as not only blind, but spiritually dead as well. Actually, it is not difficult to understand how one can live in the world and be totally ignorant of its meaning, its inner workings, or its ultimate goals and purposes.

The world offers too many distractions. People who live in our cities, for example, are astonished when they go into the country and note how many stars they can see. These stars shine just as brightly over our cities, but the city lights blot them out. It seems illogical that the feeble lights of electric signs can overcome the light of the stars, but to our earth-bound eyes, this is all the distraction that is needed.

Similarly, we all began life asking some very basic questions: "Who made me?" "Why am I here?" "Who is God?" "What is God like?" "What happens when I die?" "Does everyone die?" For various reasons we stop asking these questions as we grow older. One reason may be that we are afraid that there are no answers. This is an absurdity, because we live in a universe that is mathematically, and in every other way, perfectly rational. Therefore, there have to be rational answers concerning the nature of the universe and God.

Mainly, we cease to ask these questions because there are too many distractions in life. We can't all be philosophers, or theologians, or even simple, lifelong students. Hence in order to earn our bread, we do other things, and these seem to demand that we commit the bulk of our time, our energies, and our thoughts to our chosen vocations.

The scientist who wants to put a man on Mars is hardly in a position to give much thought as to the ultimate significance of that feat. He does not profess to know how the exploration of one planet is going to affect our total view of the universe. But increasingly, there are people who cannot and will not be distracted from the search for ultimate reality. They want to understand how every act of man and every leap into space is related, not only to the universe, but to the Creator of the universe. More than that, they wish to unite with the Creative Force at the center. They call that Creative Force, "God."

We call these people who seriously begin the search awakened individuals. It is as if there is a part of every man (let us call it his spiritual nature) that is asleep, and remains asleep in most people throughout life, from birth until death.

Evelyn Underhill, a twentieth-century English mystic, refers to the Awakening as, "A disturbance of the equilibrium of the self, which results in the shifting of the field of consciousness from lower to higher levels." In today's parlance, we might say that the awakened individual begins to live on a higher level of consciousness. I prefer the definition of an awakening as a re-orientation. Prior to the awakening, the individual feels independent and self-sufficient. He lives in the universe and feels free to either associate with other people or not to, depending on his mood. He also feels free to associate with the Creator or not to, and feels no part of the ultimate purpose of the universe. In fact, he is probably unaware that there is a purpose to the universe. Much of modern life shouts that, "Life is meaningless." Of course, if life is meaningless, the idea of the existence of God would be absurd. No one could believe in a God who would create a senseless world.

A man's awakening must occur when it hits him that there is an Intelligence at the center of the cosmos and that he must relate to this Intelligence. One day he may not even be aware that such an Intelligence exists, and the next day, he finds a passionate and compelling drive to seek out and unite himself with that Intelligence, that Mind, that which is called"God." Eckhart referred to such people as "God intoxicated men." An old fundamentalist hymn says, "Once I was blind but now I can see." The awakened person may be someone who has been searching for many years, or he may be someone who never felt any desire to search. In most cases he was not aware of what or Who he was searching for.

Now, there is a range of terminology, and as you read various literature concerning mysticism and mystics, you may find some differences in how the authors define these terms. However, among the mystics themselves you will find astonishing consistency. I will use the terms as they are employed by the classical mystics. Hence, when I state that the awakened person seeks after spiritual development, I mean simply that they are seeking an experiential relationship with God. Although not all men and women undertake such a search, all possess the potential. The mystics have taught that in everyone there is a small spark of the divine, and that it lies dormant within the individual until he is awakened. It is fanned into a blazing heat when it is awakened. From that moment on, he is a man with a new and completely different orientation. He has new values, new priorities, and he has forsaken material goals for spiritual ones. He may continue to engage in the same occupation, like Jacob Boehme, who continued to make shoes, or like William Blake, who continued to paint, but with a new purpose and with new ends in mind. Everything, to the mystic, even shoemaking, has to serve the Supreme Being, and to be done in a manner that is in harmony with the universe. The mystic and modern ecologist understand one another perfectly. However, the mystic is not motivated to fight for ecology, primarily because it is necessary for survival, but simply because it is right! It is in keeping with God's order of things.

The Awakening may affect different people in various ways. St. Paul felt it necessary to spend two years in the desert in order to sort everything out, whereas Jesus spent only forty days. Let us look and see what happened. Jesus's Awakening took place in a simple baptismal ceremony in the River Jordan by John the Baptist. At that time he was anointed by the Holy Spirit. He left the scene and went into the wilderness to begin a forty-day period of purgation.

The experience of the Apostle Paul was even more dramatic. He was traveling on the road to Damascus with documents that gave him authority to seek out, arrest, and imprison the followers of Jesus. On route, he was confronted by Jesus, whom he believed dead, and was struck down by a blinding light. The psychological shock literally blinded him for several days. He was led to Damascus and stayed there several days until one Christian, Ananias, visited him and talked with him about his experience. When his sight returned, Paul fled the city to begin, in the desert, a two-year period of purgation.

Not all awakenings are of this sudden or dramatic nature. Ignatius of Loyola was riding on his horse one day, when he noticed a tree bursting into bloom. In this natural act of Spring's awakening, he became aware of the force of God in the Universe and experienced a personal spiritual awakening.

This points up another reason why it is so difficult for modern man to relate to the cosmos. He sees so little that is natural. In urban life, he does not observe the stars, seldom sees a sunrise or a sunset, has little or nothing to do with producing food, has no association with other living things except man, and may be completely surrounded by artificial things. He may have a wrought-iron flamingo on his lawn, he may even have an artificial lawn, and in his house he is apt to have artificial flowers. His food is prepackaged, and milk comes in a carton or a can. As a child he may even have imagined that cows give cartons of milk as a hen lays eggs. We have surrounded ourselves with so much that is artificial that we have seen a real revolt against it. People have more live plants in their homes today than for several decades, and mineral specimens have become a part of the decor of homes and offices. Man subconsciously rebels against the artificiality of modern life. In a sense it almost seems as if the modern world is trying to convince man that the only things that matter are what he sees and feels. Governments and industry are content to have it that way, because then man becomes predictable and, at least, outwardly contented and docile.

The awakened man is always the unpredictable and creative individual. He tends to clash with the hierarchy of the Church and with the state and society. His values no longer enable him to blend in with the antiseptic artificial world around him. What basically has happened? It is as if a man lived in a house with, let us say, two rooms. His bodily house contains two rooms which he calls "mind and emotion." Since these are all he knows, he seeks to furnish these appropriately and meet the needs their existence creates. Suddenly, one day he becomes aware of a third room, "spirit." Its existence opens a whole new world to him. Not only is his life broadened, but he also senses that the needs of this room supersede both of the others. This is why I like to see the awakening as basically a re-orientation.

The unawakened person is headed in one direction, largely in pursuit of a self-realization which is limited to living in a world dominated by emotions and mind. Now he makes a complete, one-hundred-and-eighty-degree turn, and heads in an entirely different direction. He pursues not self-realization, not even self-preservation. In fact, he no longer values his old self, but seeks to find a new self, the one that God intended for him at his creation. Jesus made completely clear just how such a man's attitude is altered, by saying that such a person would be willing to lay down his life for his brother's sake.

If self-preservation is no longer the end of life, then something new must take its place. Simply stated, it is the need of the awakened one to unite himself with the universe and to literally lose himself in God, and paradoxically thereby to fulfill himself. The awakened soul who sees for the first time the need to unite with God begins to see his fellow man in a new way. Christ likens this experience to that of the blind man receiving his sight. Whether we call it new sight or simply a new awareness, the new proximity to God of the Awakened soul makes him aware of how far short he falls of God's perfection. He begins to judge himself and tends to dwell less on the imperfections of his fellow man. Moreover, he begins to seek in them the image of Christ and to recognize that they, like himself, are imperfect children of God. This new awareness is nothing more than that, born of a new orientation. Once we move from self-centeredness our eyes are opened, and whereas we were blind, now we can see. The effect is to transform us and make us more Christ-like.

The cults have failed to grasp the simplicity of this truth, and seek another explanation. They refer to consciousness-raising, and believe it can be induced by a set of mental exercises, rote meditation, or drugs. Often they manage to counterfeit this new insight, and we get a cult that teaches all men are innately good, and if we will only love one another, all will be right with the world.

But all men are not innately good, and unless they turn from self-centeredness to God-centeredness, they will continue to do evil; and wars, crime, sickness, and poverty will continue to ravage the world. Members of these cults often become disillusioned when they discover that ordinary mankind has not changed, but remains in a sinful state, estranged from God until He chooses to awaken them.

In contrast, the God-centered person knows how far short of perfection we all fall. But he is not disillusioned, for he looks not for a natural goodness in man, but for the goodness of Christ to possess every man. We know that God wants to lose no man, but has given to him an immortal soul, which is but a small reflection of God's goodness. It is through this soul, which is a porthole into man's nature, by which God seeks to enter and to unite Himself with us.

Our awakening shows us two things about ourselves. First, we understand how much we need God's Grace; and second, we know that to each man is given sufficient grace. If he was so inclined, this would cause him to turn from self, and to dedicate himself to his Creator in love and service. This then is the paradox. Man is free to live apart from God and yet not quite free. As long as there is that spark of the divine within himself, he must either respond to it and let it flame and become like God, or quench it, if he can, and become the complete animal.

One part of man yearns for independence, but still another responds to that force from without and within. There is a spark of the divine within, and a loving God without who seeks and yearns for him. If you desire to be united with God, you have only to accept the fact that God wants to be number one in your life. It only seems logical that He does, since He created you for His own purpose. The mystics believe that God not only wants to be number one, but unless He is, our life becomes a meaningless tragedy without true joy. Obviously, most people, and even possibly you, do not believe this. It is commonly believed that pre-occupation with God is a lifestyle becoming only to saints and would-be saints. For the rest of us, life is too demanding. We have to earn a living and give our spouses and children tender loving care. We often presume that we do not have the time to include God in our lives. We may even imagine that this would be burdensome. But the mystics, on the contrary, have found that God can make all things easier and that letting him into one's life brings perfect joy.

Can you, dear reader, believe that your life is too full and that little place remains for God? Do you feel, as do many, that God is someone you don't know very well, that because you do not know Him well, you can't conceive of how He can become the center of your life? Yet, if you profess to believe in God's very existence, you must believe He created you, and therefore there are many things which must logically follow from these first two premises.

First, your creation by God, places upon you the responsibility to know Him. How is it possible for you to have lived these many years and not to have made it your business to know him? Can you honestly believe that either your creation has no purpose, or its author is unknowable? Admittedly, finding God may not be easy. But almost everything worthwhile is not easy, and you have put more true effort into trivial concerns than you have in your search for God. Learning tennis, bridge, chess, knitting, hunting, or fishing all swallow vast blocks of our time, but the search for God is hardly given ten minutes a day. I have not even mentioned television. How many saints spend as much time before the altar as you do before the TV set? Even if you plead that you spend little time in front of the TV compared to other people, it is probably true that the time you do spend, if given instead to the search for God, would have made you one of God's most intimate friends.

There is much you can do to turn this around. The prayers in this volume can help you get started if you will use them as prayers and as a guide to your thinking about yourself, your needs, and more especially, your need for God in your life. Then too, you must look at your environment and your lifestyle. Take a look at your home, and try to understand what it says about you, your values, and your goals in life. Looking at my own situation, I discovered some interesting choices that have to be made, if my life is going to be in harmony with God. For example...

Every year, around Christmas time, our family debates whether we should buy a natural tree or an artificial one. So far, we have resisted buying anything but the genuine article. There are many reasons for our decision, and not all of them make much sense. I suppose the principal reason is that we are used to it, and it is something we associate with our childhood. It may seem a bit far-fetched to claim that one of the reasons for my choice of the natural tree is that it is one more small contribution to my awareness of God. Having an artificial tree is a kind of fraud: not very sinister, and probably almost harmless, but yet in a very small way clouding our vision so that it becomes a little bit more difficult for us to discern the truth. We find it all too easy today to substitute what may look like the real thing for the true item. Our homes are filled with artificial flowers, we eat "home made" bread manufactured by Ward Baking Company, and plastic ducks sit silently and motionless on our front lawns.

We can even go into a restaurant and not only eat foods doctored with various chemicals, but have our plates decorated with an inedible but colorful plastic parsley.

And what is the harm? If we buy an artificial tree, there will be no pine needles to clean up, and we would not have the task of searching for the perfect size and well-shaped tree that will fit our room specifications. Furthermore, it is less of a fire hazard, and finally, we would not have the annual expense that is connected with the real thing. After all, what is the difference? You can even buy an imitation aerosol scent to make your tree smell like the real thing. Who knows the difference and who cares? Many will pass by and think they are seeing a real tree and most will "Oooh" and "Aaah" at the perfect symmetry and at the colorful decorations and lights. Yet, it can make a difference. If we surround ourselves with so many things that are of our creation, are we leaving sufficient room for the things that God has created? One Psalmist felt drawn close to God simply by observing His handiwork. He said, "Sing praise with the harp to our God, who covers the heavens with clouds, who provides rain for the earth; Who makes grass sprout on the mountains and herbs for the service of men." The writer of the 147th Psalm goes on to describe the many and wondrous creations of God. Each of them excites him, and each of them helps him to become more aware of God.

If we live in an artificial environment, it is easier to lose sight of God. In fact, if we see nothing but man's handiwork, from autos to artificial trees, are we not prone to feel that the world is ours, and most of what has been made has been made by man? No wonder we are a generation devoted to the worship of self! No wonder so many complain that they do not see God, for where are the things that He has made?

One of the ways in which God makes himself known to us is through His creations. We learn from them the meaning of beauty, care, compassion, and concern. It is important that we discipline ourselves to see the wonders God has made. It is difficult to do this if we shut out of our environment many of the things He has created. Also, we can have both God's creations and man's creations about us, and by choice, choose only to see those we prefer.

What are the things that occupy your heart and thoughts: the things of God, or the things of man? It is terribly easy to substitute many poor imitations for the good things of life. As we substitute artificial flowers for the real thing, and are content with their false and inferior beauty, so also can we substitute superficial living for the full life that God has offered us.

Jesus said that He came to earth that we might enjoy the abundant life. But all too often we are satisfied with the imitations and tinsel decorations of the material life. A man who would qualify for any spiritual poverty program will proudly state that he enjoys all the best things of life. One of the great tragedies is that many people who have seen clearly that the good life does not consist of things have assumed incorrectly that it consists of cultural pursuits. But surely anyone who can see the superiority of culture to possessions can also step up to the world of the spirit.

For God would have us use and possess all things for the good of our souls. He has given man all things to use and has taught us not to settle for the trivial. Christ Himself set the example. He was able to enjoy all things with many men. He was present at their feasts. He spoke in their synagogues, and he challenged all men to see not only God's creations, but God, and to become united with Him. The way Christ offered us was to be filled with hardships and angers, but the rewards were to be everlasting. Not for Jesus and His disciples were the temporal three score years and ten, but the real and everlasting Kingdom of God, life abundant and life eternal.

Amidst all the glitter and tinsel of this life man has but to choose. God leaves us free to choose the trivial, and if we wish, to waste our lives away pursuing things that do not matter, or to seize the pearl of great price, the everlasting Kingdom of God, and the gift of eternal life.

The most common and most dangerous misconception held by men concerns the choice we are given regarding God. Most men believe they are completely free to serve him or not. In a sense this is so, but not, He would have us know, without great peril to ourselves. Jesus tells us a story in the fourteenth chapter of the Gospel According to St. Luke, making crystal clear the limitations God has placed upon our "free" choice. He says:

> A certain man made a great supper, and bade many: And sent his servant at supper time to say to them that were bidden, 'Come: for all things are now ready.' And they all with one consent began to make excuse. The first said unto him, 'I have bought a piece of ground, and I must needs go and see it: I pray thee have me excused.' And another said, 'I have bought five yoke of oxen, and I go to prove them: I pray have me excused.' And another said, 'I have married a wife and therefore I cannot come.' So that servant came, and showed his lord these things. Then the master of the house being angry said to his servant, 'Go out into the streets and lanes of the city, and bring in hither the poor, and the maimed, and the halt, and the blind.' And the servant said, 'Lord, it is done as thou commanded, and yet there is room.' And the Lord said unto the servant, 'Go out into the highways and hedges, and compel them to come in, that my house may be filled. For I say unto you that none of those men which were bidden shall taste of my supper.'" (Luke 14: 16-24)

The picture that Jesus paints is very uncompromising. "God," He says, "gives an invitation." It is an invitation that He fully expects everyone who receives it to accept. To make certain that we fully understand, Jesus gives as examples three of the most common excuses. The first is from a man who purchases some property. We all have some responsibility to the things that we possess. It is not only the very rich who are so tied down with property that they cannot find time for the things of God. Witness the number of people who put caring for the house and yard before Sunday morning worship. To possess the latest model automobile, thousands work countless extra hours, and plead that they have no time for prayer, or that they are unable to find the energy for works of charity or the support of the church. The second is even more common. They plead, "I work. I am a working man and it is hard to find time for devotional life." In most cases, we are not discussing countless hours per day in prayer and meditation. This is not what is truly necessary to know and serve God. Rather, a minimal amount of time is begrudged to the God who is the giver of all. This laborer must test his oxen, punch a time clock, or work in an office. He pleads that at the end of his labor he is too weary to devote one hour on Sunday morning to worship God. God gives us 168 hours every week, and we cannot devote one hour to Him? How ridiculous we must appear to God! If we read Jesus's story carefully, we must be aware that God does not expect us to take his invitation so lightly. Either we come, or else we are no longer welcome in His house.

Lest there be any doubt, Jesus gives us still another example. A man marries a wife, and with no further explanation assumes that surely this is sufficient reason to ignore the invitation. But the plea of personal involvement with those with whom we are most intimate is no reason to neglect God. Jesus elsewhere in Scripture puts it even more strongly. We must be prepared to forsake father and mother, brother and sister, and even husband and wife, and put God first in our lives. We are His creatures and we are subject to Him. That He wants us to come willingly, and of our own accord, is also very clear. What He does not acknowledge is that human kind would want to reject His most gracious invitation.

All men are made of two selves: the self that God has created and who desires to serve Him, and the self we have become since our birth through the influence of others and the choices we have made daily between what God wills for us and the temptations of the world we have chosen instead. And when we listen to our true selves, obedience to God comes easily, and we accept His invitation to feast with Him. But when we listen to the false self which we have created, we go our own way, pleading this excuse one day, and that excuse another day.

But God does not stand idly by, choosing instead to fill His house with other, more deserving guests. We are free only in the sense that God does not instantly compel us to do anything, and to truly live and to be a part of the world He has created. We are always compelled to obey or to forfeit our place at His table.

A man struck by this realization first becomes awakened, and then becomes conscious of his need for purgation, that he might become a fit habitation for God, and dwell in union with Him.

III.

PURGATION

What happens to the awakened self? St. Paul spoke of a blinding light which he faced on the Road to Damascus. To the awakened one, the process of coming out of the darkness into the light must seem blinding. If we accept at face value the claims of the mystics, the awakened self must now face reality for the first time. Hitherto, the individual has lived in a world that he fancied was real. Like the rest of us, he held to certain illusions, most notably the one of his own self-sufficiency, and the belief that he did not necessarily need to be linked directly to the Center of the Universe, God. Once a person has come to awareness, he must deal with the realization that everything we do must be directed from the very Center of the Universe, and must be in harmony with God. With this comes a feeling of inadequacy, guilt, and unworthiness. For the first time the awakened soul is forced to deal with a spiritual being, and that Spiritual Being is God. Not only is He greater, mightier, and more merciful, but He is of a different species. How can gold unite with dross? How can there be communion between two such unlike species? It is questions like these that throw a man into what John Epes called "The Dark Night of the Soul," but which is simply known as "purgation." For if what the awakened one sees is real, then he himself no longer is, as he heretofore imagined, the ultimate reality. The fear now exists that he is outside the circle of reality, a finite illusion in contrast to the infinite certainty.

But along with the darkness, the awakening also brings with it some light. The awakened soul realizes that man is not all dross. Within him is buried a seed of the

Divine which has, at last, been awakened. So the new reality which he now sees about him is also within, albeit in a small, insignificant amount. Purgation will enable a man to give this Divine seed a chance to develop. The awakened one becomes aware that he must prune away and weed out everything within him that prevents this seed from blossoming forth. Clearly, if he is to unite himself with the Absolute, he must rid himself of all within that is not in harmony with the real world as he now observes it.

The world that he had heretofore seen was created by man in man's own image. The strife, the hatred, the envy, the injustice was not the work of the Creator, but are reflections of himself and his fellow man. Lest we mistake this mirage for reality, we must purge ourselves of those attributes which produce the mirage. Stated in terms of traditional theology, the awakened one must rid himself of all that is "sinful." Sin is simply defined as anything and everything that is inconsistent with the harmony of the universe and stands between man and God.

Because the awakening is such a traumatic experience, the awakened man or woman embraces purgation eagerly. For now it is clear that life, up to this point in time, has been a sham. Everything a man may have done, everything he has said, and everything he has believed has been based on a false view of the universe. Seeing things from his own self-centered view, what he has seen has been distorted, and even when he had glimpsed reality, it had not been clearly perceived, but seen only through an opaque lens.

Since his dealings with other people had been based on an evaluation of them that was distorted by his own inadequacies, jealousies, resentments, and prejudices, he has been unfair and unjust. The unawakened individual tends to judge others severely and himself with understanding, compassion, and with not a little rationalization. Of his past judgments, the awakened one now becomes ashamed, and he is inundated with guilt.

Paul, who persecuted the Christians and condemned many to death, realized after the Damascus Road experience that he had the blood of hundreds of innocent people on his hands. No wonder he fled into the desert to purge himself of the guilt, of the sham life which brought these harsh judgments in the first place, and to prepare himself to live so that the divine self might have better soil in which to develop and flourish. He now wished to become Christ-like, and without purgation this is not possible. He wished to find a new self in reality, his real self, and shed the old self which had brought him to utter despair.

The old self around which the individual's entire life revolves, prior to his awakening, has all of its being in the finite material world. This "self" tends to regard material things as real and spiritual things as unreal, imaginary, or at best, unprovable. Hence, to say that material things only might be real is to say that no action should be predicated on the existence of spiritual things, since they may prove to be an illusion. Therefore, for the unawakened man it is only possible to live in the material world. The spiritual world seems too unreal, too uncertain, too much of an illusion to be trusted. Thus, it is possible for an ardent church-goer to live an entirely materialistic life. He pays some kind of lip service to spiritual things, and even professes that they are more real than the material. But in life, he trusts in his bank account, and his job takes precedence over all other commitments: church, neighbors, friends, even his wife and children. When he is buried, although he has professed that his real self, his soul, goes heavenward, he has set aside thousands of dollars to make certain that his material remains are protected by a sealed casket from the elements, air, water, and vermin. The truth is that the unawakened and unpurged self is earth-bound. Being material, it can only relate to the material world. Being finite, it sees other people only in terms of their finite qualities. Its own preservation is its primary aim, and the assumption is that all others are likewise motivated. The obvious philosophy for such a being must be to "Take Care of Number One." Not without reason, this kind of philosophy produces a world wracked with wars, injustice, and a distribution of the world's resources that allows over-abundance in one part of the world while millions starve in other parts.

Material man does not possess within himself any means to correct these evils. New social and economic systems will only be plagued by the materialism that produced these evils in the first place. As long as man is self-centered and unawakened, the law of "Taking Care of Number One" must prevail. As long as it prevails, world chaos and dissension must rule.

Before his awakening the individual may have deplored these things, placing the blame on other people and other nations, but now he must face squarely and honestly the fact that he must share the blame! His conscience, which was disturbed by war's existence or poverty's existence, is now doubly torn, since these things which he has learned to abhor are now seen as evils which he has helped bring about. Consequently, he seeks to purge himself of all that was associated with his former self. He has several motivations. He wants to unite with God, and he knows that no man who clings to that which is not in harmony with God has within him the seeds of eternal life. And he wants to cease being part of the world that produces war, injustice, and poverty, and become a part of the world that seeks to bind up the wounds of war, give justice to the world, and minister to the poor and needy.

Many mystics and religious people seek to combine their search for spiritual reality with a life of social service to the poor, the sick, the imprisoned, and other such needs of every type and sort. Unfortunately, many become so involved with treating the symptoms that they forget their search for God and soon revert to their old material selves. There is no purgation in seeking material solutions for spiritual problems. We ought not to forget that poverty, injustice, and war are the result of man's pathological spiritual condition.

In the twentieth century both A. M. Goichon, author of *Contemplative Life in the World*, and Thomas Merton, in his *Contemplation in a World of Action*, have attempted to combine the active life engaged in works of mercy with the contemplative life. In fact, it is among modern religious thinkers, this is regarded as the *summum bonum* of the spiritual life.

But for the mystic, the purpose of purgation is primarily to prepare himself for the indwelling of God. If purgation had no other purpose than this, it would be enough to justify the effort. He must cleanse his earthly temple so that it might become a fit habitation for the heavenly or spiritual. If in the process he contributes to the elimination of war, injustice, and poverty, well, "Praise God," it is no more than he would expect.

Is what he proposes possible? Even psychoanalysis does not propose to undertake such a radical and complete transformation. The most it offers is that the individual might better understand the forces that work within him, and sometimes through understanding, he might rid himself of an occasional demon. But the purgated individual proposes to rid himself of selfishness, lust, envy, hatred, anger, anxiety, and a host of emotions and fears that heretofore he has always contended were natural and therefore must be tolerated. In fact, in the view of many modern psychologists, he is attempting to lead an unnatural life. Such a life, they would argue, would probably produce demons even more terrifying than those he proposes to destroy.

Nearly two thousand years earlier Jesus suggested the same thing in a parable about a man who washed and cleansed his house and put out a demon that dwelt therein. Because his house was empty and prepared, Jesus tells us, that the first demon went out and found seven more demons even more terrifying than himself, and they all came and made their home in that man's house. Thus, the last state of the man was worse than the first. It is a warning we must heed, but Jesus did not intend to discourage us from spiritual progress. He only warns us regarding the pitfalls that await us during purgation.

Of course, the mystical life, *sans* all the attributes we have come to believe are uniquely human, would be impossible unless the purged one is able to draw upon new resources and new sources of strength. This is precisely what the mystic is searching for. He feels that if he can become in tune with the universe, the seed of the Divine within him will develop and grow and leave little room for the demons he has turned out to return. He expects to receive help from God in the form of Grace or Illumination. He has come to believe that he is not alone, and that he can and he ought to expect help from *without*. Before, he communicated only with the material world, but now he seeks to communicate primarily with the spiritual world.

Meditation for the western mystic is a means of communication with the spiritual world. He believes he can establish communication, first of all with God. It is necessary that he does this to ultimately achieve a oneness or a union with God. He also believes he can communicate with angels, saints, or mystics who have gone before him, and the various distinct manifestations of the Godhead. For the Christian, God is a Trinity of three separate and distinct persons: God the Father, God the Son, and God the Holy Spirit. He believes they constitute a unity and hence he is monotheistic, although his approach to God is as varied as are the Persons who constitute the Triune God.

To do this he must become like the Divine. This means he must purge himself of all that stands between him and the spiritual world. His orientation must be toward the Absolute, and he must cease to strive for anything for himself. In his ceasing to strive, he will paradoxically receive all he might be tempted to strive for.

As you pray the prayers of purgation, you will note that you are praying for nothing, except to be cleansed. The mystics call it "letting go, and letting God." In due time through this process the mystic receives the grace or illumination that leads to union with God.

Purgation is a long slow process by which a man measures every act, every thought, and every breath by the yardstick given to us by Jesus Christ. He ceases to compare his actions with any others, but allows every secret corner of his life to be searched out with the white hot light of God's Word. The standards are found nowhere but in the person of Jesus Christ and the sacred words of the Holy Bible.

The mystic's methods of eradicating sin are varied, depending much on the temperament and culture of the individual mystic. However, for most it consists of letting

40

one's thoughts dwell upon God, the life and person of Jesus Christ, and the wonders of God's creation. He attempts also to see God in every man and woman whom he encounters. His search was not in vain, for he found no man so vile that God's work was completely hidden from the seeing eye of the mystic. For Brother Lawrence, a seventeenth-century Carmelite monk, it was to fill every waking moment with thoughts of God, and thus crowd out the useless, the trivial, and the sinful from his life. For many of the mystics of the Eastern Orthodox tradition, the method was similar to the Eastern mantra. The "*starets*" or holy man repeated endlessly the prayer, "Lord, Jesus Christ, have mercy on me." The idea was to crowd out of the mind all that was not God.

The mystics were very conscious of the fact that if they took something out of their lives, they had to be certain to replace what they took out. Nature abhors a vacuum, and the life filled with God leaves nothing that is contrary to God to creep in.

Dr. William Pinard, a South African-born psychologist and mystic, added a new concept to the matter of purgation. He pointed out that during their periods of purgation, the mystics tended to be highly productive. They not only filled their lives with prayer, but also with creative work. They tended to work long hours, and if the devil finds work for idle hands, he has poor pickings among the mystics. Pinard's contention is that the mystics strained their minds and emotions to such a degree that they produced the illuminations which drew them further along the path of spiritual development. He labeled the period of purgation as "functioning," and insisted that the creative labor was as important as the prayer of purgation in completing the purgation and stimulating the process of illumination.

Kahlil Gibran, the famous Lebanese poet, artist, and seer, provides help to the aspiring mystic in understanding his own culpability, and thereby letting go of his resentments and hatreds. He holds that it may be true that no man can purge himself and make within himself a fit habitation for God until he has borne upon himself the sins of the whole world. While fundamentalists say, "Christ has done it for you," mystics remember He also said, "Take up your cross and follow me." But no man can take on another man's sin, until he can look upon the murdered soul and see in him one who would bring to the mystic the punishment which he, the awakened one, justly deserves. Since he may have only partially purged himself, he continues to remain an example which others can use to excuse their own transgressions. As long as he remains a murderer in his heart, or carries lust within himself, he is always a potential murderer or adulterer. In the same way, he can easily make excuses for himself. Those who would commit sins can always say that all men would do the same, if they could or if they dared. Knowing this, the mystic who seeks purgation is motivated to greater efforts, and through prayer and meditation tries to rid himself of his involvement with sin, directing his thoughts toward the Divine.

The so-called activist mystics, like the late Mother Teresa of Calcutta and Toyohiko Kagawa, filled their days with acts of mercy and prayer and did not distinguish between the two. Their work is prayer and their prayers are work. Those who persist in purgation are rewarded in time with spiritual gifts, variously called illuminations or gifts of grace. These often come when the awakened one is in the pit of despair, and may be fast losing hope that he might ever purge himself and become a fit habitation for God.

By far the most detailed description of the purgation process is written by John Epes in *The Dark Night of the Soul*, the title of which has become synonymous with purgation. Without exception, every mystic sees purgation as a necessary step, but each mystic selects a route as individual as his own personality. But whatever the route, all place a great emphasis on filling the mind and soul with the Divine. The idea is for God to take such complete possession of a person as to leave room for nothing that is not pure, not holy, and not God.

We cannot leave the matter of purgation without a comment concerning what is being purged. So often people think in terms of sins involving actions, but this is not the heart of the matter. The heart of the matter is coincidentally the heart. Every important matter has to do with the heart. When we disobey God, we are giving our love to someone or something other than God. This is contrary to all the laws of creation, for God made us that He might love us and, in turn, receive our love. And Scripture tells us that "The Lord is a jealous God." God wants our love and He wants our absolute obedience. But He does not command our obedience, but asks that we obey out of love for Him. We are ready to be united with God when we have learned to love Him, and have learned to also love His ways.

John Nicholas Grow says, "The Most perfect liberty is that possessed by God, Who can only will what is good."[1] Jesus demands that we become godlike. We can only feel truly free when we do the will of God and feel thrilled by so doing. When we do good in perfect love, we see His image reflected in us.

If the commandments are a burden and we derive no joy in their observance, we are still not free from sin, and still do not know the joy of perfect obedience to His Will. Obedience for the purged one is joy, and he who does not experience joy in living according to God's Laws does not behold the world through the eye of God. Jesus says we are blind, and, indeed, we are. There is a beautiful world of God's creation, but all too few ever see it. We also are beautiful. That is, the person God created was created in beauty. Unfortunately, most of us are still not that person, but have gone astray and created of and for ourselves another self, made not in God's Image but according to our own and our peers' taste. Through purgation, God seeks to free us from this pseudo-self, so that we might be free to live according to His plan for us. The litmus test we must use daily is not, "Am I living the Christian life," but, "Do I enjoy and am I thrilled by the Christian life that I live?" When we are truly pleased by the things which are pleasing to God, we become free to do as we please.

Jesus said, "The truth shall make you free." Free, indeed, to serve God in love, who in return will illumine the soul and fill the soul with the light of His truth and search out every dark corner. Then purgation will end, for we have come out of the darkness into the light. Then God will surely hear our prayers for illumination and for union with Him.

IV.

ILLUMINATION

Illumination comes toward the end of purgation and perhaps to some extent it might be seen as the result of purgation.

The experience of illumination has been defined in various ways, including the words, "It is as if one were coming from outer darkness into a blinding light." Primarily it is "knowing" God.

But it is a knowing that comes not from reason or from physical evidence, but as a gift. Illumination has many facets. Its basic characteristic is inspirational. Through illumination the mystic is inspired as no other individuals. Mystics who are artists and poets seem to become creative in an almost supernatural way. Illumination brings a creativity that sets mystics apart. Unfortunately, many would-be mystics lose their way when they cease to seek God, but turn away from Him to seek the gift of illumination. What they want is some kind of sign that they are close to God and are becoming truly spiritual men and women. To many people, unless a mystic receives illumination, he is simply not a mystic.

Jesus had people come to Him, asking that He show them that he was illumined. His reply was, "Unless you see signs you will not believe." These words were said with scorn, for nothing leads a potential mystic so easily astray as this seeking after signs.

The fact remains that the mystics, Jesus included, *did* experience illuminations. In the life of Jesus, the first illumination that was reported was the experience of His baptism. We are told that at the baptism, John hesitated and professed not to understand why Jesus felt the need to undergo this rite. But the Baptist was persuaded, and at the moment of immersion a voice from heaven proclaimed, "This is My beloved Son, in whom I am well pleased" (Matthew 3:17). The question arises concerning whose testimony provided the basis for this Biblical account. Was it John, or the spectators, or Jesus? Seemingly, the testimony is given, not as coming from Jesus, but from a third party. Since none of the writers of the gospels were present, we must assume that it was either John, which seems unlikely, since he was dead when the gospels were written, or some of the bystanders who later became disciples. Of course, John could have passed the testimony to some of his disciples, and they in turn to the writers of the gospels.

The best-known illumination of Jesus's, and the one with the greatest objective testimony, is the experience that He had on the Mount of Transfiguration. Jesus was traveling along the coast of Judea near Cæsarea Philippi, when the question of his identity arose. Who was He? There were many rumors flying about. Some thought He might be a prophet newly returned, such as Elias or Jeremiah. It was at this time that Peter affirmed that He was indeed the Christ, the Son of the living God. Six days later, after a discussion of this question between the disciples and Peter, Jesus, Peter, James, and John ascended what was described as a high mountain. At this time Jesus was transfigured before them. We are told, "His face did shine as the sun, and his raiment was white as light. And, behold, there appeared unto them Moses and Elias talking with Him." (Matthew 17: 2-3)

This illumination was unusual, in that the outsiders there observed not only what happened to the mystic, Jesus, but also witnessed the appearance of other spiritual figures from the past, Moses and Elias. They were convinced by what they saw and heard that they were on holy ground, and they urged Jesus to remain there. They offered to build shrines to him, Moses, and Elias.

Jesus discussed this with them, and a second and even more remarkable event took place. A bright cloud appeared and they heard a voice saying, "This is my beloved Son, in whom I am well pleased; hear ye him"

(Matthew 17:5). They literally fell down on their faces and were afraid. Jesus assured them everything was all right, and urged them to descend the mountain and to tell no one about their unique experience. Apparently, the discipline of the group was very strong, because we have no record that anyone revealed this event during his lifetime. It must have been a great temptation, because the disciples were under constant pressure to prove to many people that Jesus was, indeed, called of God. When and under what circumstances Peter, James, or John shared this with anyone else we cannot be sure. However, the account appears in Mark's gospel, so presumably Mark heard the account from Peter.

Biblical scholars are certain that when Matthew wrote his version of the gospel, he had Mark's testimony as one of his sources. Jesus was very typical of all mystics, in that he told the three followers not to reveal His experiences to anyone. There are many reasons why mystics are reluctant to discuss their experiences of illumination, but the primary one is that the mystic cannot explain what has happened, feels no need to, and is certain that the events would be misinterpreted by almost everyone. There is another very strong reason: a very strong conviction that one should not speak about the incident. We may call this a mental block or simply an innate sense of propriety, but some way and somehow the experience does not seem a proper subject for public discussion.

Take for example, the experience of one modern mystic. One day on a drive through a southwestern desert he saw at a distance Christ appearing in the heavens. It was so vivid that he instantly picked up speed so that he might observe the people in the car ahead of him. Did they notice what he was seeing, or was this only for his eyes? He never did find out. He reported that the apparition remained for probably five minutes and then was replaced by the figure of a naked woman. This too lasted for some time, and again he has no way of knowing whether he saw this alone, or whether the occupants in the car which he passed had also witnessed it. Also, the images were so clear and so vivid that he felt they must have been visible for miles across the desert.

What did he make of this? Like most mystics, he wants to remain silent. He feels it is too easy to give the experience the wrong interpretation. The one feeling that he felt deeply was that while he was seeking Christ, his life did not measure up to Christ's high standards of personal purity. This is hardly material one would want to share with others. But in any event, he never doubted the experience, although a year later he came to an entirely new interpretation. His first interpretation caused him to become more devoted to the woman with whom he was living. A year later, another experience, more prosaic but not less traumatic, caused him to see that he was being asked to choose between Christ and the woman. He made the choice, and subsequent events convinced him that the highway experience pointed in that direction. Again, why share the experience? For him, it was a life-changing event, but it had no meaning or value to anyone else, other than the knowledge that such experiences do occur, are real, and enormously effect the lives of those who experience them.

One more example. This same individual experienced a period of awareness of others' needs that disturbed and frightened him. He found that as he talked with people, even those with whom he was not close, he was anticipating their problems. It was almost as if he had been given information concerning them about which they themselves were unaware. A man known to our subject, an artist, who had been engaged for several years on some murals that are destined to be national treasures, ceased his work because of some criticism by the people in the community. At no time did the man share with him any significant details concerning the criticism or his reasons for quitting the project. One day they met in the village, and it was as if everything about the painter that could be known was known to the subject. After the conversation was over, the painter said that he was going back to his work to complete the project. He credited our subject for seeing his work in a new light. Yet, hardly a dozen sentences concerning the work had passed between them, but each sentence hit its mark, because the needs and the concerns of the artist were exposed.

After this incident, the awareness of other's needs disappeared, and to the best of my knowledge never returned with the same force to the subject. However, this is very typical. These illuminations come and go, although as the mystic matures, they come with increasing frequency and remain a little longer each time. Many mystics become despondent when they lose these powers, and in their striving to regain them, risk losing everything. When they become reconciled to seeing God for His own sake, and not for any good that may be derived from Him, the Illuminations recur.

St. Teresa of Avila gives us additional reasons why we should not seek after these illuminations. First, of course, is that we should never seek after God from any motive of self-interest. Secondly, it is our pride that causes us to think that somehow we can do something to merit these gifts. Thirdly, we have Jesus's emphasis that the truly spiritual person knows it is more blessed to give than to receive. As Teresa puts it, we ought to seek out suffering in imitation of Christ rather than seeking after gifts. Fourthly, she says that God is not obliged to give us illuminations. Fifthly, she says very simply that our striving will be in vain. She states that there is no conduit through which these gifts come, that we receive them when we go to the sources, to the living water that is Christ.[2] In our search for illumination, we need to be reminded of Jesus's injunction that, "He who would save his own life will lose it, but he who would lose his life for my sake will find it." It is not the search that has brought these illuminations, but the process of purgation, and it appears to be God's way of aiding the mystic through a most difficult experience. Through illumination God reaches out, giving the seeker hope and strength.

In addition, Evelyn Underhill says that purgation opens up a whole new view of reality. What was heretofore obscure now becomes clearly visible· The illuminated individual sees nothing that has not always been there, but as Underhill phrases it, "He is able to apprehend another order of reality."3

God's Kingdom now assumes the reality that the earthly world has heretofore had in the person's consciousness. No longer is there a groping, and a blind search for the Kingdom of God. It is *here*, and it becomes the ultimate reality. The illuminated person is still a long way from Union with God, but he no longer has a single doubt concerning the superior reality of the spiritual over the material world.

There is also a greater ability to understand and respond to the leading of the Holy Spirit. Obedience to God's Laws, which had been so difficult, now through Grace becomes easier, and it is disobedience that becomes increasingly difficult.

But more importantly, the still small voice within becomes easier to hear and to comprehend. Life day by day has more direction, and God's tender leading is more clearly felt. The soul no longer has to consciously seek direction, but is aware as never before of how earnestly he seeks to do the will of God. It is as if he no longer has a will of his own, for God has become his all.

The illumined man is not self-self-conscious about his new higher plane of existence, but his focus is ever on God. Now God is more clearly revealed and His Will is ever more readily known. More importantly, the illumined soul is aware that his new insight is not of his own doing, but is is a gift from an all gracious and loving God.

V.

UNION WITH GOD

When Meister Eckhart quotes God as saying, "I became man for you. If you do not become God for me, you do me wrong,"4 he was talking to a world that was unified in its concept of the nature of God. Today, even within the Church, there is little agreement concerning the nature of God. "God," a student in one of my classes years ago told me, "is a force. I don't think it is a person." If what the student says is true, then what is called "union with God" is not possible.

Much of the religion espoused by the new cults and the Eastern mystics is of this impersonal variety. The Eastern mystics seek to empty man of self, desires, and drives. This, they believe, will lift him to a higher state of consciousness.

It is presumed that this higher consciousness is within. Nothing is expected from the Person Christians think of as God. Such cults seem to believe that man can be helped by beings called "avatars," "gurus," or whatever, who possess powers unknown to ordinary men. These men claim that they can transmit these powers to more ordinary mortals. Often a price is attached to it, but then, if one receives value, why complain? Obviously, the new gurus have a lot of customers who aren't complaining. The fees asked for by Scientology, Transcendental Meditation, and others may run up into the thousands. They claim to offer all the "benefits" of Christianity, except one. Of course, Christianity does not promise any benefits, except that of eternal life. Jesus, held out the hope of sacrifice, suffering, and persecution to his followers. Hence, it was not the Church, at least officially, that claimed that the faith offered benefits, but rather objective observers outside the faith.

Some of the gurus do suggest that they have within them eternal life. The hitch is that they all die. This usually, but not always, causes their followers to seek out another guru, lose the faith, or await the return of the dead guru. Followers of Meher Baba say that he "dropped the body" in 1969, just short of his seventy-fifth birthday,"[5] and they wait to hear from him in some new reincarnation. For the moment, the fact that they wait seemingly in vain has not cost them many followers. The reason for the tremendous following of the Meher Baba's and the hundred-odd gurus is very simple. They claim to offer what the mystics have found, but without sacrifice, and completely divorced from the Establishment.

The no sacrifice claim is peculiar, because once you get into one of the new cults, you find they demand almost total allegiance, and tremendous sacrifices of time and money. Compared to the demands of the cults, the Establishment is a penny ante beggar. But as pointed out earlier, the organized Church in the fifties and sixties seemed to support the very materialism many people were seeking to escape. It was felt by many who turned to the cults that the Church talked about spiritual things, while practicing materialism and lending its institutional strength in support of a repressive and materialistic society. Most persons, though fortunately not all, failed to distinguish between the Church as an institution and its teachings. The strange paradox is that the mystics for the most part had difficulty in gaining the acceptance of the organized Church. Even today, the Church's new mystic, Thomas Merton, was accepted only with reluctance.

The mystics are people who not only teach about eternal life, but seem to have found it through union with God. To them, God is a person. They contend that God and man are of the same genus. As we have seen from Merton, they view man as having two natures: a false self and a God-created self. In a sense, Merton argues that man does not unite with God, but that God seeks out the created self and pours Himself into man. The whole process of purgation is to purify man so that the refined self, like God, can be united with God, who is also like pure gold.

The mystics, particularly Boehme, used this analogy frequently. "Gold," they said, "does not unite with dross but only with pure gold." Hence, purgation is a refining so that man and God can be of the same "golden" substance, and can merge and be completely and perfectly united. When man becomes like God, he is transmuted from man to the Divine Essence. He becomes one with Him, because, at this point, God seeks him out and unites with him. This is deification, if you will, but it does not mean that the personality is lost. Neither does it mean total and absolute identification with God. As God and Christ are both one and yet different, so the mystic is one with God and yet different.

The mystic does not seek to be equal with God, but seeks rather a spiritual marriage. And like an earthly marriage, the partners are one, but not the same person, or even equal persons. To seek oneness with God is not to seek to become as great, as powerful, as omnipotent, or as omnipresent as the Almighty. To seek oneness with God means, primarily, to submerge our wills in His. To love what God loves is to be united with Him in the best and greatest sense. When a couple becomes one, it is because they share all things that matter. Even more, they share the same values. This is not to say that union with God does not bring about tremendous changes in the mystics. These changes are radical, and constitute the objective evidence that such oneness has, indeed, been achieved. What are the changes that overtake the mystic united with God? First, all sense of sin disappears. What does this mean? Fundamentally, it is evidenced by the lack of a judgmental attitude toward others. The mystic has no desire to sin, and hence, does not feel compelled to condemn those who do sin. It is illustrated in Jesus's attitude toward the woman taken in adultery.

Jewish law decreed that a woman taken in adultery must be stoned to death. Who would do this? You might answer, "Society," but that begs the question. Who in society could bring himself to kill another person? Not the righteous, for they would be adverse to killing. It would have to be a member of society who felt threatened by this woman's action. If we see our sin in her, and deny our sin, we would tend to judge her harshly. Jesus said that they who were without sin should cast the first stone. Why? Simply because such a person would not be tempted. Jesus, who was without sin, was not tempted, and did not feel threatened by this woman, and therefore could sympathize with her. He certainly did not condone adultery, as is evidenced by His advice to her to "Go and sin no more."

Jesus's action was not one of indifference, but he was never moved by the misconduct of others to strike out and avenge their sins. Even to those who would take his blood, he showed no feeling of condemnation, but only feelings of compassion.

Secondly, the mystic has no fear of death. He reacts to death as he does to sin. It has nothing to do with him, so he does not have the same emotional response to it that ordinary men have. Since he has the assurance of eternal life because of his union with God, threats to take his life leave him unmoved and unafraid.

If we read the account of Pilate's encounter with Jesus, we must draw the conclusion that it was Pilate who was afraid. He washed his hands, symbolically, in a public act that was politically harmful to him, but he did so out of fear.

Finally, the mystic seems singularly free from selfishness, envy, hatred, possessiveness, in fact, from all the things that separate the rest of us from God. Because he is no longer plagued by desires that cannot be fulfilled, or torn by envy, bitterness, and hatred, his state can be described as dwelling in the Kingdom of Heaven.

Characteristic of the mystics who have achieved union with God are some attributes which seem almost superhuman. The mystics seem to have been lifted beyond the cares of this world. The most striking is the loss of the fear of death. We are so accustomed to thinking of this fear as a normal reaction, that we stand in awe of anyone who does not react to a threat to his life with great fear.

54

Yet, once a person has been united with God, if only for a moment, all fear of death is removed. This is the best evidence we have that a person has been truly united with God. It is a certain sign that he has received the gift of eternal life. The mystic tends to be unconscious of the fact that the fear of death has left him, for he has ceased to care whether he lives for the moment or forever. All he knows is that he lives for God. This is sufficient. It is both a quality of the mystic and evidence that the mystic has truly been united with God.

Of what does this oneness consist? It cannot be a marriage of unlike substances, for such a thing would be a contradiction. Before the soul can unite with God it is purified in fire, so that all that is not Deity dies and the seed of eternal life is all that remains. The self that emerges is not new, but has been hidden by a false self that man adopted in contradiction to God's wishes. Once this false self dies, the self that God created at the mystic's birth takes over and is ready to receive the Heavenly Bridegroom. From henceforth the two shall be as one. Like any marriage, the two shall maintain their separate identities. Husband and wife are one, yet both do not give birth to young, and both do not possess equal power to hunt or to lift heavy objects.

In the mystical marriage, God alone has power and God alone is the Creator and Sustainer of life. The mystic is not God, he is wedded to God, and he is one with Him. Meister Eckhart must be forgiven for some exaggeration. Yet, it must be granted that once a man has become united with God, he no longer can be solely man. He has become Deified, and although he has risen above the angels, he is not equal to the Uncreated God, but is subservient and rejoices in his subservience to God. There is no contradiction here, but there is a mystery. To dwell in close intimacy with God is Heaven enough. The soul united with God is free from sin, and the desire for sin. Having perfect peace and fulfillment, it seeks after nothing that its Love does not also love.

This state is not one of unbroken bliss. One of the things that happens to one in union with God is that one becomes concerned for all mankind. He has found God and now wants all others to find Him. Consequently, he learns of the disappointment experienced by God and the frustration caused by man's infidelity. He sees mirrored in other men, his own long history of rebelliousness. Therefore, he relives his own failures and misdeeds, although it ceases to matter. He finds himself in the position of Jesus, who when he had done all he could to bring the gospel to the world, and especially, his own people in Jerusalem, upon seeing the city from the hills wept for her.

What union also brings is new life, and a joy beyond our present understanding. The mystic has undergone a transmutation. He no longer fears death, and the joy and peace which surrounds him are always a mystery to those whom he meets. Some have described this state as euphoria that has no reason or basis. The mystic may be in prison, under penalty of death, but seems untouched and his joy undiminished. Those who threaten him sometimes become frightened and sometimes seek to hasten his demise and increase the suffering in the process of his execution. The reason is obvious: the joy stems from a source unknown, and is not experienced by his persecutors.

The mystic is lifted beyond the pain-pleasure principle. The joy is so intense and so unrelated to external reality that it causes transfiguration. The fact that union with God can and does occur rests upon a great cloud of witnesses who have seen this transfiguration happen in the lives of hundreds of men and women historically labeled as mystics.

The reaction of the witnesses is varied. Some have scoffed, a few have understood, but all have realized that they stood in a Presence. Every mystic in union with God reaches this peak, and is less aware of it than those who observe him. One of the great distinguishing features that sets the mystics apart from modern day gurus is the humility of the mystics. They do not seek to convince others of their divine attributes, but often deny having anything not possessed by other men. They claim nothing, but obviously possess much. It is important in researching the lives of spiritual men and women to pay less attention to any claims they may make, and rely on the observations of objective witnesses.   The astonishing thing about the mystics is that often their persecutors are the first to recognize their Divine nature.   Pontius Pilate, who was not a friend of Jesus, felt he had to wash his hands of His death, before he condemned Him to death upon the cross.   Something about Jesus caused him to be afraid.

It is an exciting and awesome thing to stand before God and those He has chosen as His saints.   But seek nothing less than to come into the Presence of the Living God.   As you pray the "Prayers of the Mystic Way," seek to know, to love, and to serve your Creator.   For Jesus has given us the key to eternal life, and it is this: "Seek ye the Lord and the Kingdom of Heaven and all the rest shall be added unto you."   And He said also, "He that seeketh his life shall lose it, and he that loses his life for My sake and the Kingdom, shall find it."

VI.

PRAYERS FOR THE MYSTIC WAY

Dear Reader,

I trust you will not use the prayers that follow until you have read the preceding pages and have diligently studied the great devotional classics. For without some understanding of the four-fold path of mysticism, these prayers may not be of any help to you at all.

This little book of prayers is intended for those who have studied such writers as Meister Eckhart, Jacob Boehme, and Thomas à Kempis, and who wish to follow them in their spiritual quest. Many of you are just mildly interested. You have not experienced an awakening, but wish that you might have such an experience. Nothing has happened to stir within you such a passion and longing for God that you will set everything aside and seek Him. There are others who can tell you better than I, how and to whom such awakenings come. My only contribution is the awakening prayers. Jesus repeatedly said, "many are called but few are chosen." If you are among the chosen, these prayers, if said faithfully, will in God's own time contribute to your awakening.

If after sufficient time, you do not acquire a thirst for God, it might be well, before concluding that you are not chosen, to seek to purge yourself of your sin. Jesus said, "The pure in heart shall see God." To purge without acquiring a desire seems, at first glance, to be an impossibility, but it is likely that a heart and soul can be so encrusted with sin that an awakening is impossible. If the prayers of purgation arouse within you a feeling of repugnance for yourself, you might return and pray anew for an awakening. The awakening, of course, will make you even more counscious of your sinful state. You will want to cleanse your soul of all that makes it an unfit habitation for the Lord. This is by far the most difficult step in the mystical path. A cursory reading of Augustine's *Confessions* and Boehme's *Confessions* will demonstrate the extreme pain and difficulty involved in the purgation.

We cannot, without the help of God, become pure and holy. There is little we can do but humbly and earnestly petition God for our release from sin. "Stand aside!" says Eckhart, but even this step requires the help of God. If ever a man must pray without ceasing, it is in this step. Consequently, over half of the prayers that follow are devoted to purgation. Daily we must live the prayer, "Create in me a clean heart, O God, and renew a right spirit within me."

Only when we are purged of sin can we expect the illumination that comes from God. The purging need not be complete; indeed, it probably cannot be completed until the soul is stimulated and aroused by the lure that comes with illumination. Man must catch a glimpse of heaven before he can gain strength and resolve to leave the world of the flesh. We seek these glimpses not for themselves, but because they will lead us to the union we seek with God. The illuminated soul must pray for union, for now he stands on the threshold waiting to fulfill his destiny and to unite with Almighty God. We cannot win our Lord with prayer, but we are impelled by the excitement within us to give voice to our hopes and aspirations. Knowing that God will enter every soul that is prepared to receive Him, we must ask Him to come and to make His abode with us. It would not do to take for granted a gift so precious and a God so gracious. What is not our right, and but is an undeserved and generous gift, must be asked for. We must ask, if only to remind ourselves that we have not earned a single precious minute of life. Yet, if we prepare ourselves to receive Him and ask in the Name of Jesus Christ, God will humble Himself that we may dwell in unity eternally.

I beseech you, dear Reader, not to tarry a moment but accept the privilege of prayer and prepare yourself to accept the greatest gift of all, a God who seeks you, even as you seek Him.

PRAYERS FOR AWAKENING

I.

Heavenly Father, teach me the meaning of my creation, that I may serve the purpose for which I was made. Bring me to Thee, O my Creator, and teach me Thy ways, lest I lose myself in the complexity of this life ere I discover the glory of the next. Amen.

II.

Hasten, O Lord, the time when I, like all men, must realize that the day of reckoning is at hand. Unless I find Thee soon, time will run out and my life will have ended before it has begun. Bring me to repentance that I may turn to Thee and to Thy paths of righteousness. Amen.

III.

In my search for Thee, O Lord, help me that I do not lose myself in a selfish concern for my own salvation. Neither let me forget that I, myself, urgently need Thee, as well as those for whom I offer prayers of intercession. Cleanse me, O Lord, that I may not be ashamed to come into Thy Presence. Amen.

IV.

Heavenly Father, the path I have trod is so well worn that I have difficulty in changing my course. Thou who has never tired of calling men to Thee, call me now with the insistent voice of a father to a child, and give me the courage to heed Thy urgent call. Amen.

V.

Heavenly Father, help me to understand why the trivialities of this life so engross me that I do not earnestly seek Thee. Perhaps if I understood their great attraction for me, I could be free of their temptation that takes so much of my time, energy, and resources. I find time for everything but Thee. I implore Thy forgiveness and pray that above all, Thou will implant in me an irresistible desire to seek Thee. Amen.

VI.

Gracious Father, forgive my unbelief. I have never known Thee and I fear I never shall. Stir Thy Spirit within me, that I may be moved to seek Thee without ceasing. Amen.

VII.

Heavenly Father, much of my life is spent and I have never seen Thee. Nor have I ever known anyone who has seen Thy Countenance. Yet logic tells me that Thou must exist, and if Thou art real, those who are pure in heart surely must be allowed to see Thy Heavenly Visage. Have mercy upon me, O Lord, and before this feeble belief departs from me, make Thyself known, that I might behold Thy great Glory. Amen.

VIII.

Lord, Heavenly Father, Thou knowest that though I profess belief in Thee, it is an empty profession. If I truly believed, I would be so awed by Thy Greatness that I would anxiously seek Thee. Yet, Thou knowest how seldom I seek Thy Presence, how irregular are my prayers, and how seldom I worship Thee in Thy House. Give me a belief strong enough to alter my way of life. Amen.

IX.

O Heavenly Father, why is it that I make so little effort to find Thee? Surely my doubts do not explain such great indifference. I must know that if Thou does exist, this tremendous fact should dominate my every thought, word, and deed. Yet, I hardly make any effort to determine whether you exist, nor do I really seek Thy presence.

Help me, O Lord, that I may not only accept the idea of Thee with my mind, but that my heart may be so gripped by the very thought of Thee, that I do not cease to seek Thee until I have seen Thy Face. Amen.

X.

Heavenly Father, teach me not only to seek Thee and Thy Kingdom, but to create in me a desire to be used by Thee as Thy instrument for bringing all men to Thee. Above all, let me never cease searching for my Creator, lest I pass through this life without having fulfilled the purpose of my creation: to live eternally in humble and obedient service to Thee. Amen.

PRAYERS FOR PURGATION

I.

Heavenly Father, forgive me those sins whereof I am ashamed, and instill within me a desire for Thy righteousness, that I may turn away from sin and seek Thy forgiveness and salvation. Amen.

II.

Heavenly Father, because my sins are those of indifference and self will, they do not greatly disturb me. Increase my understanding of Thy will, so that I shall not fail to appreciate the simple fact that I have often turned my back to Thee. Save me from my folly and lead me to Thy saving Presence. Amen.

III.

Heavenly Father, create in me a desire for holiness that is greater than my desire to give free reign to the sins of the flesh and the mind. Help me to drive out the evil that inhabits my body, mind, and soul, and so prepare a dwelling place for Thy Holy Spirit. Amen.

IV.

Heavenly Father, I fear that it is almost too late for me to find Thee, ere I must leave this world. Help one who has passed the prime of life, by giving him the strength to forsake sin and seek Thee. Restore unto me sufficient vitality that I may pray without tiring and to know Thee, so that in contrast the world of sin will appear as dross. Strengthen me, O Lord, before it is too late. Cleanse my heart that it may become a fit dwelling place for Thee. Amen.

V.

Heavenly Father, I was created to live according to Thy law. Help me to follow in the path of Thy Son, Jesus Christ, and to live always according to Thy dictates. In His Name. Amen.

VI.

O Lord God, the enormity of my sin weights heavily upon me. Not only have I hurt myself, but each and everyone of Thy creatures has been hurt by my wanton and irresponsible disobedience to Thy commands. As no sin is private, neither is my salvation. Help me, O Heavenly Father, for the sake of my fellow man to purge myself of the disease of sin. Amen.

VII.

Heavenly Father, I know that nothing is more contagious than sin. Cleanse me, lest I infect others. Make me, instead of a carrier of the world's disease, part of the cure. May Thy healing hand cleanse me and through me others. Restore health to my soul, let I perish and lest others perish with me, and because of me. Amen.

VIII.

Lord, Heavenly Father, I have said, "It doesn't matter what I do, if I do not harm anyone else." Impress upon me that no sin is ever committed that does not harm all of mankind. By my sin, I have held back the coming of Thy Kingdom. By my sin, I have made it easier for my brother to stumble. By my sin, I have kept Thee at a distance. By my sin, I have contributed to the world disease by infecting others. Purge me, O Lord, and make me clean, lest I destroy not only myself but others, include those who are near and dear to me. Amen.

IX.

Lord Heavenly Father, let me forsake my evil ways, not because of fear of punishment, but because I have learned to love Thee and to love Thy ways. Teach me to love Thee, even as Thou lovest me. Amen.

X.

Heavenly Father, give me strength to take the first step by renouncing some act of disobedience. Help me to put down a temptation that has often defeated me. Lift me out of the mire one step at a time. Help me to crawl that I might walk. Let there be no sin so great as to defeat me forever. Redeem me, Lord, before it is too late. Amen.

XI.

Heavenly Father, I have long since learned that the punishment of my sin often comes in the form of the evil that other men do unto me. I have yet to live that others might see my goodness and turn unto Thee. They see my evil and use it to justify their own misdeeds. It has been said that the murdered is not unaccountable for his own murder and the cuckold for his own betrayal. Let these thoughts weigh upon me, a sinner, that I might yet repent and spare myself the punishment that is visited upon sinners by their fellow sinners. Teach me Thy ways that the world may yet be free of sin and the punishment of sin. Amen.

XII.

Heavenly Father, it becomes increasingly obvious to me that while I seek to find Thee, I also flee from Thy presence. I do not understand this fear to know Thee, for Thou hast shown Thyself merciful, gracious, and good. If it is Thy Goodness that I fear, remake and re-mold me that I may learn to love that which is good and be set free from my love of evil. Amen.

XIII.

Heavenly Father, teach me Thy Commandments. So often I feel that I do not break them, because my knowledge of them is so inadequate. I claim that I do not bear false witness, yet I am sure that I have said things about others that would not pass Thy scrutiny. Teach me to speak well of others, and to guard my words that I may never have to doubt whether my words are pure in Thy sight. Amen.

XIV.

Lord, Heavenly Father, I ask forgiveness for those whom I have hurt. When I have broken Thy Law, I not only sinned against Thee, but I have also inflicted pain upon my fellow man. Yet, I feel neither remorse for my sin, nor do I yet realize that my brother feels pain even as I do. Help me, O Lord to see the enormity of my sin that I may repent for Thy sake and for the sake of my fellow man. Amen.

XV.

Heavenly Father, my path through life takes me past every temptation, and because of my feeble resistance, I succumb to each and every one. Forgive me and strengthen me that I may walk in holiness all the rest of my days. Amen.

XVI.

O Heavenly Father, save me from the hatred which consumes my soul. Let not evil passions destroy the hope that is within me. I thank Thee for revealing to me that without love, I dare not even approach Thee. Cleanse me, Lord, that I may know love and peace. Destroy the evil within me that my soul may enjoy that peace and love which would make it a fit habitation for Thee. Amen.

XVII.

Give me no peace, O Lord, until I have burned out all that festers and is sore within me. Make me clean so that I can face Thee without shame. It pains me, O God, to think of how I would blush in Thy Presence because of my sin. Make haste to help me, O Lord, and make clean my heart within me. Amen.

XVIII.

Heavenly Father, Thou hast said that the sins of the fathers are visited upon their children unto the third and fourth generation. Cleanse me so that my children and my

66

children's children may be spared the punishment of my sins. In Christ's Name. Amen.

XIX.

Heavenly Father, my sins are blacker than pitch, yet my heart is not heavy. A wiser man than I would make his peace with Thee, this hour, but I continue foolishly and unafraid. When I implore Thee for forgiveness, I say that, "I am sorry," yet my claim is actually a wish. It is that I desire to feel remorse that never comes. I know that I will never mend my ways unless I recognize the enormity of my sin. Help me, O God, to see my sin through Thine eyes, that my sorrow may be great enough to bring about true repentance. Only then can I merit Thy forgiveness and find strength to mend my ways. Amen.

XX.

Heavenly Father, it seems that the pull to the world and the flesh is so much greater than the attraction to Thee. Since I cannot believe that Thy power is second to any, I am at a loss to understand. What defect within myself is responsible for this? Help my understanding, but above all save me from myself. In Jesus's Name. Amen.

XXI.

Lord, Heavenly Father, I speak of seeking Thy Presence, but cannot be certain that this is my earnest desire. Neither am I certain that I would turn from my sin in order to dwell with Thee. How can I be sorry for my sins when in my innermost thoughts I deem them small and inconsequential. Teach me the enormity of my offenses and lead me to true repentance. Strip me of my rationalizations, my excuses, and my indifference. Create within me the desire to live according to Thy Will, and bestow upon me the knowledge of what is right and holy. Above all, O God, stir up within me a hunger and a thirst for Thee and Thy Righteousness. In Jesus's Name. Amen.

XXII.

Oh, Heavenly Father, the ease with which I sin frightens me. So quickly can I lose Thee forever. I can not be certain of another opportunity to reconcile myself to Thee. Teach me to repent my ways, O Lord, and help me that I may sin no more. Have mercy upon me, for life is short and my feet hasten not after Thee. Amen.

XXIII.

Lord, Heavenly Father, I ask forgiveness for those whom I have hurt. When I broke Thy Law, I not only sinned against Thee but I also inflicted pain upon my fellow man. Yet, I feel neither remorse for my sin nor do I yet realize that my brother feels pain even as I do.

Help me, O Lord, to see the enormity of my sin that I may repent for Thy sake and for the sake of my fellow man. Amen.

XXIV.

Heavenly Father, my path through life takes me past every temptation and because of my feeble resistance, I succumb to them all. Forgive me and strengthen me that I may walk in holiness all the rest of my days. Amen.

XXV.

O God, save me from the hatred which consumes my soul. Let not evil passions destroy the hope that is within me. I thank Thee for the knowledge, that without love I cannot live with Thee. No, without love I dare not even approach Thee. But cleanse me, O Lord, that I may know peace. Destroy the evil within me that my soul may become a fit habitation for Thee. Give me no peace, Lord, until I have burned out all that festers and is sore. Make me clean so that I can face Thee without shame. It hurts me, O God, to think of how I would blush in Thy presence because of my sin. Make haste to help me, O Lord, and make clean my heart within me. Amen.

XXVI.

When strong passions stir within me, forget me not, O Heavenly Father. For unless I can be aware of some greater power outside of myself, I will surely succumb to the flesh.

Inspire me to a vision that is higher than all the temptations of this world in which I dwell. Amen.

XXVII.

Lord God, who hast promised that the pure in heart shall see Thee, save me from the temptation to believe that there is any other way. Make clean my heart within me that it may be a fit habitation for Thee. Purge me of all that is impure, and make my deeds pure, my words as pure as my deeds, and my thoughts as pure as my words. I know, O Lord, that I have not seen Thee face to face, and yet I find excuses. I long to see Thee and yet do not remove the impurities that blind my eyes and dim my vision. Teach me, O Lord, to face up to this simple truth, and strengthen me by Thy Holy Spirit, that I may become a pure spirit and be worthy to gaze upon Thy Countenance. In Jesus's Name. Amen.

XXVIII.

Lord Heavenly Father, Thou has promised forgiveness to all those who truly repent their sins. Help me to have true repentance and grant me Thy pardon. Make clean my heart within me, Lord, and create in me a desire to keep myself pure and holy all the rest of my days. Amen.

XXIX.

Lord, Heavenly Father, help me to enjoy a life of holiness and righteousness. Teach me not to look back to past sins lest I mistake nostalgia for remorse. Teach me to live in the present and to wholly commit myself unto Thee and Thy Will. Amen.

XXX.

Heavenly Father, teach us to conduct ourselves so that Thy Ways may prevail in the world. We often plead that the world engulfs us, yet, it is a world of our own making. It lacks peace, we deplore it, but we ourselves are not peaceful.

Teach us Thy ways, O Lord, before we help create a world even more hostile to Thy goodness and peace. Amen.

XXXI.

Heavenly Father, sin is an ugly word and I shy away from it. I know others sin, but I call my own sins, mistakes, or even argue that they are not at all what they seem.

Help me to distinguish right from wrong and to tear from my vocabulary such terms as "righteous anger," or "it is only natural," and "we are only human." Strip me of my excuses and false reasoning and teach me to face my sins and repent. Amen.

XXXII.

Heavenly Father, draw closer to Thy servant that Thy closeness may strengthen my determination to serve Thee. Give me strength to overcome the sins of the flesh which threaten to overwhelm me. Cleanse my heart and my mind that I may dwell in purity and holiness all the days of my life. Amen.

XXXIII.

Lord, Heavenly Father, teach me to enjoy the blessings I have received at Thy hands. Save me from dwelling upon past hurts by others. Teach me to consider those hurts as just punishment for my sins, so that I may know that I have atoned for them and accept my absolution. Let me live this day according to Thy will, Thy truth, and Thy holiness. Amen.

XXXIV.

Lord, Heavenly Father, I acknowledge that I am sinful and unclean. Cleanse me, O Lord, and set me free from the bond of iniquity.

From evil desires, Good Lord, deliver me.
From thoughts that disturb my soul save me,
   O Lord.
From hatred malice and spite, cleanse me,
   O Lord.
From the desire to seek vengeance upon
   those who have harmed me, Good Lord,
   deliver me.

Grant me, O Heavenly Father, freedom from temptation, release from vengeful thoughts, and Thy Peace which passeth all understanding. Amen.

PRAYERS FOR ILLUMINATION

I.

Lord, Heavenly Father, remember the emptiness of the soul that has been purged of sin. Without the Light of Thy Illumination, the soul is a dark void inviting all manner of evil spirits to make their habitation within.

Lighten the darkness of my soul by the Illumination of Thy Spirit. May I become an instrument of Thy Light and be used for the creation of Thy Kingdom here on earth. Leave me not in darkness, O Lord for I long to dwell in the Light of Thy Countenance. In Jesus's Name. Amen.

II.

Lord, Heavenly Father, do not let me be like those who seek after signs. If illumination comes, may I value it not as a sign of Thy approval but as an invitation to seek Thee more fully. Illumine me, O Lord, that I may see those things which Thou has in store for me. May the revelation of Thy great power draw me ever closer to Thee. Amen.

III.

Heavenly Father, Thy World is pleasant even for those of us who sin against Thee. Since we are surrounded by pleasant experiences, it is difficult to forsake this world for Thine. The pleasures of this world are so well known to us and the joys of Thy world are still a mystery.

Illumine us, O Lord, that knowing something of the joy that is to come, we may be inspired to forsake our earthly pleasures for the Greater Joy that is to come. Amen.

IV.

Lord, Heavenly Father, when I am away from Thee, I am in utter darkness. Draw me nearer to Thee, O Lord, that my soul may be illuminated by Thy Heavenly Light, that I may see clearly the path where Thy Holy Spirit would lead me. In Jesus's Name. Amen.

V.

Lord, Heavenly Father, grant that we may seek heavenly things, not alone for our soul's salvation, but more especially that we may become instruments of Thy Peace, and that we may serve Thee in leading men to Thy Heavenly Kingdom. Amen.

VI.

O Lord, I seek not after signs but after Thee. Brighten my path, Lord, by the Light of Thy Illumination and beckon me to enter into Thy Kingdom. Without Thy guiding light, O Lord, I am lost. In the darkness which surrounds my soul, O Lord, I have often strayed from Thy path and need a beacon light to find my direction. Illumine me, O Lord, before I come to accept my state and lose the desire to find my way. Illumine me, O God, before it is too late. Save me, O Lord, by Thy most timely Illumination and make me Thine forever. Amen.

VII.

Lord, Heavenly Father, life is but toil and pain when thou art far from me. My soul is in darkness and longs for the Light. Illumine me, O Lord, that I may not grow fearful in the gloom which surrounds me. Drive out the darkness, with the Light of Thy Illumination. In Jesus's Name. Amen.

PRAYERS FOR UNION WITH GOD

I.

Heavenly Father, help us as we seek to follow in the footsteps of Thy dear Son, Jesus Christ. Sanctify us, that we may be one in Christ, as Thou, Father, art in Christ and He in Thee. Grant this, O Lord, unto us all so that we may dwell in unity now and for evermore. Amen.

II.

Lord, Heavenly Father, when you created this world you were not satisfied, for loneliness plagued you even as it plagues man. In order to have fellowship you created man in your own Image.

I, too, have experienced loneliness and it cannot be quieted by any but Thee. I seek Thee, Lord, even as Thou hast sought me. If I have been found worthy, come and dwell in my heart and permit me to dwell in Thine that we may be one, even as Christ is One with Thee. Grant that we may dwell in unity, forever and ever. Amen.

III.

Heavenly Father, I thank Thee for all Thy gifts to me. For the gift of life and for Thy constant and tender Protection. For Thy forgiveness of my many sins. But above all, I thank Thee for the moments when Thou hast torn aside the veil that I might see the glory which Thou hast prepared for me.

May I not rest until I have made Thy Kingdom my home. For until I become One with Thee, even as Thou art One with Christ, I am nothing and cannot be counted as a child of Thine. In His Name, I pray. Amen.

IV.

Lord, Heavenly Father, you did not create me in order that I might die. If I am to live as you have intended, draw nigh to me. Apart from Thee I cannot live, yet, I cannot come nearer to Thee on my own strength. If we are to be One as Thou and Christ art One, it is Thou Who must bring this about. I wait, O Lord, I wait. If I am lacking, O Lord, show me my failing. If I am qualified, receive me unto Thyself. Amen.

V.

Lord, even though I would hide from Thee, seek me and come and dwell within me. Though my struggle to prepare my soul as a dwelling place for Thee has been irregular and totally without merit, it has exhausted me and left me discouraged. I know I cannot earn Thy love or the right to be eternally with Thee, yet my heart is frustrated because of this. All I can do is ask, and I am ashamed because I am unfit. If I can be refined and cleansed, do it, O Lord, by whatever trial of fire will accomplish the purging and will overcome everything within me that is inconsistent with Thy Presence. In Jesus's Name. Amen.

VI.

Heavenly Father, show me the way to Thy Heart. I dare not approach Thee without Thy leading, for the union which I seek is not my right, nor is it anything that I deserve. It is mine, even as life is mine, possible only by Thy most gracious gift and continued only by Thy forbearance. Grant to me what I dare not ask, do not deserve, and cannot earn: the gift of eternal life with Thee. For it was for this that I was created that I might dwell with Thee, Thy Son Jesus, and the Holy Spirit, now and forever. Amen.

NOTES

CHAPTER III

[1]Grow, John N. *Spiritual Maxims*. Springfield, IL: Templegate, 1961, p. 15.

CHAPTER IV

[2]St. Teresa of Avila. *Interior Castle*, Garden City, NY: Image, 1961, p. 84.
[3]Evelyn Underhill. *Mysticism*, New York: E. P. Dutton, 1961, p. 233.

CHAPTER V

[4]Evelyn Underhill. *Mysticism*. New York: The Noonday Press, 1955, p. 420.
[5]William J. Peterson. *Those Curious New Cults*. New Canaan, CT: Keats Publishing Inc., 1975, p. 199.

BIBLIOGRAPHY

Anonymous. *The Cloud of Unknowing*. NY: Harper & Brothers, 1948.

Baker, F. Augustine. *Holy Wisdom*. New York: Harper & Brothers, undated.

Blakney, Raymond. *Works of Meister Eckhart*. New York: Harper & Brothers, 1941.

Boehme, Jacob, ed. by W. Scott Palmer. *The Confessions of Jacob Boehme*. New York: Harper & Brothers, 1954.

Bucke, Richard M. *Cosmic Consciousness*. New York: E. P. Dutton, 1941.

Butler, Cuthbert. *Western Mysticism*. London: Constable Publishers, 1951.

Cheney, Sheldon. *Men Who Have Walked with God*. New York: Alfred A. Knopf, 1945.

Gibran, Kahlil. *The Prophet*. New York: Alfred A. Knopf, 1928.

Goichon, A. M. *Contemplative Life in the World*. St. Louis: B. Herder Co., 1959.

Graef, Hilda. *Mystics of Our Times*. Garden City, NY: Hanover House, 1962.

Hamann, Johann G. *Werke*, 5 vols. Vienna, Austria: Thomas-Morus-Presse, Im Verlag Herder, 1949.

Kepler, Thomas, trans. *Theologica Germanica*. New York: The World Publishing Co., 1973.

Merton, Thomas. *Contemplation in a World of Action*. Garden City, NY: Image Books, 1973.

_____. *New Seeds of Contemplation*. New York: A New Directions Book, 1961.

_____. *The Seven Storey Mountain*. Garden City, NY: Image, 1970.

Otto, Rudolf. *Mysticism East and West*. New York: Meridian Books, 1964.

Petersen, William J. *Those Curious New Cults*. New Canaan, CT: Keats Publishing, Inc., 1975.

St. Teresa of Avila, translated by E. Allison Peers. *Interior Castle*. Garden City, NY: Image, 1961.

INDEX

www.ingramcontent.com/pod-product-compliance
Lightning Source LLC
Chambersburg PA
CBHW021348090426
42742CB00008B/775